DIMENSIONAL

ASCENSION

Multi-Dimensional Living for Light Workers.

© Copyright 1995 Jules Kennedy

Book number one of the Utopian Vision Ascension Series

DEDICATION

I dedicate this work and this message to all those who support beauty, love, and life everlasting.

Preface
WHAT IS CHANNELING
By Jules & the Guides

We all channel, all of the time. We bring thoughts into verbal and written expression continuously. Where do these thoughts come from? And why do we choose the ones we do to individually express?

Thoughts are simply threads of energy comprised as matter. Thought is the initial component of material manifestation. "What you think is what you get." Through the process of meditation and other methods that quiet the mind we begin to clear away enough clutter so that thoughts of higher quality (of finer vibration) can enter our mental bodies. Thus *channeling* (this is a process of obtaining information of a higher sort via going into a semi or full altered state of consciousness—a state of trance to some degree—and voicing verbally the messages sent from other life forms in consciousness) of seemingly outside energy sources can occur.

Here is an explanation of channeling by the guides:

It may seem as though, when one is (so called) channeling, that information is being sent in from an outside energy source. This is only a perception, as it is not possible for anything to come from without the Self, for everything is the Self. And yet the Self is nothing. This is quite confusing for the rational mind to understand.

The energy patterns that you call the guides are only outside of your personal perception. We shall use the term "personal perception" in reference to that which you perceive yourself to be. You are "so big" in your perception and you are no larger, no smaller. You are who you are at any given moment in perception. You may perceive yourself to be intelligent one day and perfectly stupid on another. These are definitions of perceived Self. They are not the actual Self.

However in attempting to define the process of channeling to you, we must work with your limitations. We understand and acknowledge that you do know everything and that you have chosen to forget knowledge in order that you may play a fun little game of discovery, of remembering. It is to our liking also for we have chosen to play along with you.

You see, in actuality, we are a part of you that you have forgotten. It has been since the beginning of humankind's evolution that those choosing to listen to more than the mass consciousness voice have heard other voices. You have historical records of profound statements made by prophets and seers from all times. Why is it that these persons seem so wise and able to interpret or hear such high information? It is because they have chosen (either consciously or subconsciously) to expand their perception of consciousness.

Visualize in your mind's eye your own consciousness. See it. Notice how large it is. Perhaps it extends hundreds of feet beyond your physical-ness or perhaps just a few feet. Within this consciousness is everything that you know, everything that you can retrieve at will. Say two plus two equals four. This you know and can retrieve instantaneously when asked. Now there are many things hidden within this perception of consciousness that are not readily visible to you. Perhaps you are attending a theater presentation and you can recite the lines to the play before the characters themselves recite them. This could be due to the fact that you played Romeo in an earlier high school performance, or that you read Shakespeare many long years ago and had forgotten.

Now if we were to tell you that you have the potential ability to recite each and every word that any given person were about to speak, it would scare you into submission wouldn't it? Yes, that it might. But we do express to you that you have these abilities and humankind is on the brink of discovering profound "telepathic" (we use this word sparingly for we have not found appropriate description in your language for the process of mind-linking) abilities that are possible in all advanced stages of consciousness.

We shall expound upon the abilities of consciousness in further discourse. We wish now to explain the process of what your society defines as channeling:

Channeling seems to those who are experiencing it to be a process by which higher information is accessed. When one is developing consciousness, he or she is in actuality just opening up to remembering parts of consciousness that have been forgotten.

When human evolution "fell" into the density of *third-dimensional consciousness*, (the perception of third-dimensional consciousness is about all that is seen from human awareness--in this consciousness everything is solid and there is nothing beyond what can be known through the five senses) all other dimensions were temporarily forgotten. Let us play with this for a moment. Imagine in your mind's eye that you have no physical-ness. You have no physical body, no material possessions to maintain. Do you sense how light filled you are, how you have nothing to take care of?

When humankind made the choice to descend into third dimensional perception, they also chose to do it perfectly. And to do density with such perfection, it is all but impossible not to get lost within the physical-ness. It takes all of one's time and energy just to maintain materialism. For those of you trying to "get out", take a good look around at how much materialism you are attempting to maintain. Does it take much of your time? Yes? Well then you will never get out until you take on a lighter perspective and clean up unnecessary materialism. We do not say this lightly however, for it is a serious subject.

Let us take a look at many who state that they wish to channel or expand their personal consciousness. We look at their homes and we see clutter, massive clutter. We see unnecessary boxes of material items, which will most likely never be used again. Why would one wish to hang on to clutter, which serves no personal use? It only gets in the way of expansion. One must have a lot of empty room to move into. Such is the void in consciousness. First one must clean out the physical closets, thus proceeding with massive clearing of the emotional and mental closets.

There are many processes by which to clear the emotional and mental baggage that humans carry. Find an appropriate method, which seems to eliminate the darkness in the most expedient way. It is not always necessary to know exactly what garbage is being thrown. For often it is best not to know. But it must be done to clear the way for light to shine through.

Because humankind chose to experiment with density, it was necessary to develop belief structures that would maintain and keep (set up) the physical structures of 3-D. For example, in order to keep traffic moving smoothly you must have your stoplights. In order to keep your physical shelter you must maintain the electrical and plumbing features. It is necessary to make repairs in order that the structure be maintained. We suggest however that there are many structures that no longer need maintaining (such as outdated relationship units no longer appropriate to personal expansion.)

We are also suggesting that many cling to obsolete ideas of what the Self is, of its capabilities. Often you do not acknowledge the incredibleness of your abilities. All that is necessary is a willingness to see, to experience. We tease you with this note for we know of your curious nature. You are much like your feline, for you will curiously explore all of your perceived reality. We lead you then teasingly into this discourse. So be it that you will discover massive amounts of fun and exciting insights that you will experiment and play with.

We encourage you to take a very "light" look at much of what will be revealed to you in this book, for you need no more heaviness in your world. You need only light to make the next leap in consciousness. We express our sincere gratitude to those of you who are reading this. You can bring guidance into your personal consciousness. This guidance is more expanded than you presently know. Just by opening up spaces, by clearing out the old unusable baggage that you carry, you will begin to feel energies of varying quality. This will enlighten you into higher more expanded states of consciousness. And soon you will become the guidance that you once channeled. Isn't this a marvelous experiment that we together and singularly have created? We hope that you feel the excitement of this, our adventure. We have much information to share and wish to have it charged with the energy of you the reader. For each individual representation of spirit has a piece to give, a part to play.

Reactions to the following material will vary. You may read through the material quickly and easily or it may take you quite some time to work through it. Some readers may decide this information is not appropriate to their way of living in this world. It is not meant to preach but to share another version of a possible truth. This truth is working in my life and the lives of many others who have read this and other books within the *Utopian Vision Ascension Series*.

Dimensional Ascension: Multi-Dimensional Living for the Light Worker is followed by a workbook. The book is subdivided into sections. At the end of each of these sections you will be instructed to follow up with workbook questions. The page number where you will find these questions will also be listed. The workbook can be used individually or in study group process. Or you may decide not use them at all. For more instruction on how to use the workbook, please see page 92.

TABLE OF CONTENTS

INTRODUCTION
By Jules

This manuscript is written in pieces. When I channel, the information tends to come through in small increments. *The guides* (my spirit guides are the voices that I sense when I am in an altered state of awareness—each guidance source offers a different take on the same information or has new topics to discuss—it's as if I have subdivided all of consciousness into these seeming outside information sources so that I could better dissect and understand the deeper aspects of living within earth-human form) have told me that they give the reader only enough information to digest for the moment. They do not wish to overwhelm us. It is not necessary to have a lot of information on any given topic for "life is simply very simple." We as humans tend to make life more complex than it need be.

I began channeling back in 1990. I was working for a large non-profit organization that was putting in an entirely new computer system when I started the position. I had never worked with a computer before so it was a challenge for me to begin such a demanding job and also acquaint myself with the computer. I chose to stay in my office several evenings per week after everyone had left to practice my keyboarding skills. Of course, by the end of every grueling workday I was in quite a tired, altered state of mind. I was not paying attention to what I was pounding out on the keyboard. I was only there to practice. In fact I do remember closing my eyes on occasion just to allow my mind a rest. Little did I know that I was being prepared for a channeling session. One evening as I sat at the computer with my eyes closed, a seemingly strange, but familiar sensation came over me. It felt as if someone else was there yet I knew this energy sensation well. It had been with me as a child and felt very comforting. It began to speak through me onto the keyboard. I allowed it to continue for many an evening after the first. But soon I became my own worst skeptic. I began to read what I was channeling. Things like "everything is love, everything is light, and everything is comprised of frequency." "Now wait a minute," I remember thinking to myself, "this stuff is spooky." It confronted the entire reality of density and darkness of which I had created for myself at that time. It opposed everything I was living. So I took all of the typewritten channeled material, put it in a red folder, and hid it in a drawer at home, not to remember it until two years later.

In the meantime I began studying and practicing a metaphysical course working with the *light body* (this is an invisible energetic body that can extend tens of feet out from the physical body—it is a body that can be developed through work in meditation; working with energy, frequency and light through visualization can strengthen and make this body useful to the light worker). The course started to change my life. It wasn't until midway through the course that I discovered the hidden red folder. I opened it and began to read. The information I had channeled two years prior was exactly the same as that which I was learning presently in the light body coursework. How was it that I had the ability to channel information at the previous time having absolutely no understanding of it, but now I was studying it from another teacher, another source? This has since been a great cause of excitement to me. I rarely question any more the enlightenment that comes to me when I channel, for inevitably I begin to live every passage. It is my hope that you too will start to experience wonderful changes in your life as you read through this material. This channeled data often has transformative effects upon the reader. Words are the energetic formations of soul symbols recognizable to the intellect, felt by the heart and actualized into experience by the human body.

Personally, I now explore the communication coming to me from perceived outside sources as simply an expanded state of consciousness that I have chosen to view as being outside of my present Self. When I began channeling, my guides gave very basic information. They would give me advice about my personal life, i.e. which book to read, which person to call. They would even lead me to places (through visualization or by physical sensation) I'd never been in order that I could interpret the energy. These guides seemed outside of me at the time but today they are what my conscious person has become. I regard this communication as the spiritual guidance that helps me live peacefully in this world. I share with you the wisdom that has been imparted to me via the channeling process. Each and every person will have a different response to the material. This is what makes planet earth a special place. Individuality provides for a unique cohabitating world in which to live. Variations on interpretation of the same message allows for the possibility of an integrated and diverse experience for each individual soul living in human form.

When I incorporated these personal guides as part of "I" it then became necessary for me to explore even more expanded knowledge; knowledge that was relevant to many people upon the planet instead of information that pertained just to my personal well-being. It was not long before guidance was coming through from a guide named Talemahe'ke (Tally, as I sometimes refer to her.) Tally is a very feminine energy source, which comes to me from the *fifth dimension* (in this dimension the light worker can begin to use light to shift perceptions and actual life experiences—Tally uses the fifth dimensional vibration of grace to do her work). She tells me that she is able to step down her vibration and that I am able to step up my vibration so that we can meet in the fourth dimensional energy spaces. It took me a while to maintain a sense of fourth dimensional perception in order for me to channel Tally for any length of time. But today it is very easy for me to BE Tally's energy. I now wear her energy often, but not completely. I still slide in and out, but I am coming very close to becoming that (her) energy expression. What I mean by this is that when I channel I go into an altered state of consciousness, much like the stage just before falling asleep. I can still feel things and am totally aware of my surroundings, yet I can feel things that are sensually beyond what I normally feel in my everyday, waking consciousness. At first Talemahe'ke's energy felt outside of myself, something foreign to how I normally felt. It did feel wonderful but different. The longer I worked with Tally's information and energy in meditation and put it into practice in everyday life, the more I began to feel that she was a part of me. I took on her wisdom as a part of who I am in everyday life. Therefore, I no longer feel that her voice is a separate part of consciousness outside of me. She has become a component within the whole of me. Talemhe'ke will speak to us "On Becoming Grace".

My next move in consciousness was to become one with the energy of The Twelve. They came to me completely by surprise one day as I was channeling with a friend. It was as if Talemahe'ke stepped aside, leaving a wide-open space for this intense new energy to come through. The Twelve speak about all kinds of issues relating to consciousness. They span the entire spectrum of the twelve strains or dimensions of consciousness that are possible for us to reach while in the physical plane of consciousness. We are capable of incorporating, and thus utilizing, these twelve dimensions. Presently we only use energy from the first four dimensions and often (for most on the earth plane) only the first three dimensions.

The Twelve has come to assist us in remembering our abilities of utilizing much finer dimensions in *frequency* (the sensual rate at which you feel your body or something else vibrating—as with most of the information in this book, frequency can be felt only as an intuitive understanding and can't be measured by scientific methods at this time) in order to create a possible Utopia; Heaven on Earth. It is the destiny of the earth plane dimension to move into Heaven and become Heaven. It will only be through our personal and planetary willingness to expand into extensive layers of consciousness (with the assistance of the guides and aware human life forms) that we will shift the entire consciousness of the planet.

The Twelve is a Master Consciousness for which I have great respect, although I will also become this consciousness. We shall all become this consciousness. So it shall be said that The Twelve keeps me on the edge of my own consciousness. It keeps me in suspense as I continue to push out the boundaries of my own conscious spaces. It has become great fun to play with consciousness, to experiment with where frequency and light can take me. The Twelve encourages all of us to play with consciousness in whatever way seems exciting to each individual. Find the things that fascinate you about the mind, the body, the spirit, the emotion, and the planet, and research these pieces in depth. When we understand one piece we can understand the whole. The Twelve will expound upon the different layers of consciousness. It is my understanding that excerpts from The Twelve will comprise the majority of this manuscript. It is essential that their information be presented to the earth plane at this time.

It was only a brief period of about two hours, approximately six months prior to writing this that I had an encounter with an energy source labeling itself as the Naguda Force. I was alone, channeling The Twelve on tape, when the Naguda Force was introduced to me by The Twelve. Now it seems to me that the Naguda Force was very impersonal and impatient. The energy of this guidance was difficult for me to maintain at the time. The Twelve told me however that it would be necessary to complete this manuscript with information from the Naguda Force. The Naguda Force will speak to us about Metaphysical Earth Changes. These are not descriptions of the physical changes per se that the Earth herself will be going through, but will be very poignant information describing the social/spiritual evolutionary changes about to take place as the Earth plane shifts into fourth and fifth dimensional living.

Future sequels to this book will discuss in depth the extreme changes, capacities, and experiences that are forthcoming on planet earth.

From that one brief encounter I had with the Naguda Force, it was my experience that there is no emotional component to this energy. As a highly emotional human being myself, it was difficult for me to perceive living my life without emotion. Although the Naguda Force is not a physical living entity (I perceive it as one energy when I channel it, but it refers to itself as "we" in the plural sense), I was exposed to the energy through the channeling process. It felt very stiff, cold and heartless when I began to bring it through. The Naguda Force seemed unfamiliar and calloused somehow. It was hard for me to accept that eventually I may become this consciousness that seemed without emotion. This particular strain of consciousness is knowledge, strictly information. The Naguda Force tells me that it comes straight from the Akashic Records to bring the necessary information into the earth plane consciousness.

Last, but definitely not least, I will introduce you to a favorite energy source, which I have recently had the pleasure to meet. These three little fellows call themselves The Pleiadian Brothers. Their energy reminds me of little elves or nymphs. They are very lively and came to me via a dear friend. He does not channel but can feel their energy. It was during the middle of one night when The Pleiadian Brothers approached me. Their energy was so vibrant and alive that I had a hard time communing with them at first. So I asked my guide Talemahe'ke to speak with them and interpret for me. This was yet another fun experiment with consciousness and channeling for me, and it worked.

My interpreter Tally informed me that the Brothers were in actuality the guidance force for my aforementioned friend. They explained to me through Talemahe'ke that I would be a channel for their energy and that they would speak through me to the earth plane on the topic of love and compassion.

Since my first encounter with The Pleiadian Brothers, I have been able to maintain a more consistent connection with them in order to bring the information through. They inform me that the frequency of love has been jumbled and mis-communicated (mis-transmitted) on the earth plane and it will take some undoing to accomplish complete, pure, and total love. It will be the information provided by the Pleiadian Brothers that will complete this manuscript. I hope that you, the reader will enjoy the spaces that this information takes you to. I also hope that you will be able to find or sense your own personal and planetary guidance. For that is the next step in this our evolution together. We all must pay attention to the guidance, which will expand our consciousness. I wish you well and happy reading!

Chapter 1
A WELCOME FROM THE GUIDES!

Welcome to a unique journey through time and space, one which will be enveloped within your being to such a degree that you will never leave the ascension path. We welcome you, we the Pleiadians, Talemahe'ke, the Naguda Force, and The Twelve to this manuscript of power, of peace, of pleasure, and of ambiguity. It is ambiguous because it speaks not only truth but of ridiculous constructs (willful false testimonies of mankind) that have been concretized, solidified into seeming reality, and developed into form on your planet, such that it limits your exploration. Therefore we are here to assist you in destroying those constructs (those illusions and false truths) that hold you back from your true nature. We speak only truth because truth is all that lives on. And our message will live on in your hearts and your minds until you become this message, this experience.

Ascension is simply an experience of totality. It begins with an intellectual understanding of completion. Or it begins with a heartfelt sense of that wholeness. However you wish to play this game is fine. We do not instruct, we only suggest. As you read these words or listen to them, you will either first understand them with your mind or you will first feel them with your heart. We do not want to interfere with your learning process but we do insist that the time in history is approaching when you must open your hearts and your minds to the ascensional shift in consciousness. It is happening and you can no longer prolong it. It has been prolonged already. It is now time for this shift.

If you choose to not pay attention, you will lose the experience. And what an experience it will be. We suggest that you do not want to lose this experience for it is magnificent. It does not matter if you have been preparing for a long time or if you are suddenly jerked awake—you will feel the incredible experience. You will experience the ascension. You are moving from your third dimension in awareness to a primarily fifth dimensional. The things you will see may appear to you to be strange, but only because you are watching with third dimensional vision. You must learn to accept from the more expanded parts of your consciousness. You can no longer sit in denial. It won't be possible. Your denial will move very quickly when you are presented with phenomena that cannot be explained from your third dimensional position.

We love each and every being on your planet but we love from our perspective, which is presently beyond your comprehension. So, generally, humankind is not aware of our love. It is experienced however by those who are becoming aware of their multi-dimensionality. We do not speak of the kind of love you feel from your third-dimensional perception. Our experience is different. It is a love that is free of judgment and discernment. It has wings of its own and carries us wherever we may be in consciousness. You will experience a sense of loss as you review this manuscript. The loss is the tangibility of your previous third dimensional consciousness. You will not be able to reach out and grasp what once was touchable.

You will not be able to hold onto old concepts. You will not want to hold onto old concepts of reality. You will lose very quickly if you do not move very quickly. We suggest that you surrender your personal will to that of the Divine will. Your will essentially is the Divine will. You may have taken a fragment of that will through the human form and made it your own. You have possessed it and have had it possess you but it is not who you are and it does not carry your entire essence. If you align your will and allow it to be integrated into the higher will, the Divine that is, then you will come to have dramatic changes in your being and in your experience. You will no longer understand the limitation, for there is no limitation. You will go and explore beyond what you have previously known and held onto. Holding on is what will get you in trouble. Material things may be removed from your possession, for when they possess you they are no longer a helpmate in your process.

You will move exceedingly fast and will grow much to your surprise. It is now time that those whom you have assumed would not wake up will wake up. If they have not chosen to leave this planet before now, they will wake up or leave very quickly. Many souls will be leaving the earth plane in search of different experiences in other forms of existence. Also, you may begin to see that another perception of earth is appearing. There may soon be evident two versions of earth reality. One earth will be the old world that humankind has dwelled upon for eons in time. The second earth is evident to only those humans developed in and that have understanding of multi-dimensional perception. It is the new earth that can be perceived and solidified only from an ascended state of consciousness. On this new earth there is no recollection of death and decay, only life everlasting in various forms.

Before your year 2012, all those who have not opened at least one spiritual eye to these changes will be leaving in one form or another. And, as a light worker, you'll understand this leaving process but you won't waste your energy trying to wake up those who have checked out of their bodies. They will be the working robots that will move you to the next stage in your planetary growth. The transition between here and there will need robotics (at its basest level) to assist you in letting go of your previous ways of operation to the more ascended ways of functional reality. Your ascension will rapidly take hold as you close the old millennium and enter the new. We suggest that you prepare your hearts for great expansion. Hatred will become obsolete. Grieving will become obsolete. Pain will become obsolete. You will no longer be able to martyr or victimize your way into the future. You will let it go, for it will serve you not. You will no longer be able to play your games of pity and sadness and sorrow. For they serve you not. You will reside in joy, ecstasy and the rapture that is. So Be It.

See workbook questions for "Introduction to Ascension".

Chapter 2
INTRODUCTION TO GRACE
By Talemahe'ke

My name is Talemahe'ke. We are drawn together, my energies as fifth dimensional consciousness and your energy as multi-dimensional consciousness. You, in your physical form, are asking to understand the multi-dimensional placement in which your consciousness resides. I can be of assistance in this understanding; but I can only relay partial comprehension of the total sum of multi-dimensional consciousness. I label myself Talemahe'ke so that you, as individual Light Worker may understand that I too create an individual being in form. However, I am solely fifth dimensional form whereas you come from third-dimensional consciousness that embodies the totality of multi-dimensionality, but operates primarily from only awareness of the physical realm.

You, through the use of your conscious mind activity, within your third dimensional form, can extend yourself beyond third dimensional awareness into as many dimensions as twelve and beyond if you were to explore further. In order to do this it will be necessary for humans residing on the earth plane to become reacquainted with the energy of grace. Grace is a necessity in overcoming and transcending that which you might label as negativity. The density that holds you to earth is no longer necessary, but because you are a complex being made up of mind, body and soul, your programming, your prior patterns encompass negative thoughtforms and experiences. Grace as an energy will help you transform your depression and your oppression. It is possible to take an angry individual and mellow such individual into a joyful state of being. Joy is contagious. And the contagion property is grace. We will use grace to blend and intermix all of the negativity into bliss.

You may be, right now, in a blissful state of consciousness. If so, begin to dwell on the bliss. Begin to feel the bliss in your body, within your heart, and especially within your solar plexus. Your solar plexus is where your heart and soul must meet. Your human heart has the capacity to go beyond the physical and become a spiritual connector. Your heart connects you as individual human to spirit, to all that is. It connects you to love, and love in its entirety is made up of grace. Grace in the fifth dimension is pure, divine frequency. It is unpretentious and knows no evil. Grace is delicate and harms none. Grace is beautiful and deceives no one. Grace can come to you by simply asking the powers that be to fill your soul with grace. Hail Mother, grace be with you. All of your prayers have asked for grace, have asked for the delicacy of being in a blissful state. That is your craving on your earth plane. That is why you search and cry and beg for opportunity to feel the graces that exist. You no longer need to feel. You need to experience and become your state of grace. Graciousness has been bestowed upon you. You have my blessings and you have the blessings of God. You are the Divine Creation and you do create divinely. It is so that your male and your female are separate because you have deemed it necessary to be separate, to see both sides of the experience. Now it is time to look beyond your simple form. You are not male. You are not female. Dis-identify yourself from your sex and become a Divine Creator with God. As you read this you will experience in one way or another the essence of grace. You may experience changes in your outer experience or you may experience changes within your inner perspective. It is guaranteed that you will have changes, experience blissfulness. You will talk to others about your experiences and the experience itself will expand beyond yourself. That is the glory in the graces. You need not intellectually understand this conversation. You need to feel, you need to experience, you need to become what God has you becoming. Your expression will become less verbal and more energetic. Your experience will become less painful and more positive. You will see the smiles on the faces of those whom you reveal yourself to. You won't need to push your way into the experience of another. All you need do is be and accept yourself as Divine.

The grace will come to you as you sit in your Divinity, as you allow. Grace simply is. Grace extends itself and allows you to walk upon it so that you may extend yourself. Grace can become a physical manifestation of energy. It is malleable. It is penetrable. Yet it is solid. Do you see the grace? Do you feel the grace? Have you become the grace? If so, go forth and extend yourself to others within the grace. If you have yet to become the experience, that is fine too. In the becoming you are strengthened and you are blessed with more of the grace. There is no hurry. But there is a time limit. If you want to enjoy the process of becoming, you must start now. If you want to wait until there is no other choice but grace on this earth, then you must wait. If you choose that you do not want grace at all, that is fine as well but you will find much difficulty in doing so on the earth plane, for she already is the experience of grace and she will allow you that opportunity. But soon it will not be an opportunity, but a necessity. You will no longer be able to maim and kill and violate one another. That will not be possible. It will not be allowed. There is too much light entering your planet and too much blending of the opposites. You will experience ecstasy in your sexual/sensual union with one another. May it be one, two, three, four or more unions they all will become one with God, one with All-That-Is. And it will be grace that brings you there. Blessed Be.

See workbook questions for "Understanding Purpose

".

Chapter 3
CONNECTING WITH YOUR SOUL
By Talemahe'ke

My name is Talemahe'ke. I come to you on this day to bring great joy--a rejoicing of all souls. The conscious connection has been made between the realms of third dimensional existence and that beyond dimension.

It may seem now an easy task for a personal connection to be made with spirit. And thus it is so that we make it available to you. To access beyond that which you already know is being made a simpler process. It will be very easy for you now to make connection with your Higher Self, or as we shall call it Power. This is not a power that is higher than you. It is a power within you.

When you have physical impediments such as illness or energy blocks, it is true then that spirit has a more difficult time entering this space. Therefore physical and emotional healing is very necessary, but not to the extent that some of you believe. We of spirit take great pride and rejoice when you are enticed or recognize the pleasure of being one in the physical plane. Therefore those things that you deny your physical body, those things that you may consider evil or destructive are not necessarily so. It is what you do with them in thought that creates destruction. If one is to choose an obsession to feed an inner void, then yes, it is destructive. But if it is done in pleasure and it nurtures the spirit, then do so in pleasure. And know that you honor spirit.

It is time in your dimension that you realize what toll the physical body has taken due to some mental structures that were set up many eons ago. It is not necessary to force or push the physical being into productiveness. All that you do must be done with ease. Therefore if a task does not come to you with ease, release it. If your soul dimension would still desire the task to be accomplished, then the soul dimension will create an easier way for the deed to be accomplished.

Honor in your being what you call a feminine essence: the essence of receiving. This is a profound gift of spirit. It is a side of your own being that has been shut down for eons. It was the challenge of nature to shut this down in order that you may rediscover it and truly know the power that it is. There is a structure that goes with a receiving nature. It is a structure of surrender. The energy pattern of surrender is very open. If you can imagine a hole filled with light, then it is within this hole that you will receive those messages that will honor your true essence. There is no such separation between what you call your Higher Self and your personality self. They are meant to be one, in fact they are one. But it is the imbalance of the masculine energy pattern in your culture today that allows for this separation to appear.

In order to honor, to reinforce, to strengthen the feminine energy patterns of which I speak, allow yourself to be much like a child. If your child needs attention, then honor that request. This may be difficult for some, but it is extremely necessary for the planet today that you be an adventuresome soul and demonstrate to others how wonderful it is to care for Self in a proper way. There is no need to feel guilt when taking care of Self. Feeling guilt can be very destructive to the soul connection.

It is extremely difficult for the spirit world to understand why it is that you abuse yourself by not taking care of Self. It is extremely difficult for us in the so-called Spirit realm to understand why it is that you do not honor Self. It is not through others that you will honor Self, it is through the Self. As you begin to honor Self you will find that other beings will honor you as well.

There is an old Native ritual on your planet that significantly honors the feminine Self. As you sit in meditation allow the visualization of a circle of light just above your *crown chakra* (chakras are wheels of light that invisibly circulate around seven primary areas of the body—there are many smaller chakras throughout the body as well—the crown chakra is about two to three inches above your head and allows for spiritual information to be received). First of all, please look at this circle, this plate, and ascertain whether or not it is open, closed, or partially open. It will be your duty to open this circle in order to allow your Soul to speak directly to you. Your Soul is meant to reside within the area of which you may call the solar plexus. This is the home of the Soul. The solar plexus is waiting for its owner to come back within the structure it has built.

It may be that you have closed the crown. If this is so you must work at opening this circle and enlarging this circle so that your soul may more easily enter your body. It is also necessary to visualize the energy with which you resonate. Visualize this energy leaving through your feet as you walk upon the earth. It is important that we do not dispel this energy. We must honor the earth and give her back what she has given us. Therefore give your energy to her when you walk upon her. She will give back many times.

I have one last item to speak about. It is important that you determine your belief systems about what you call love. Love is not at all that you believe. Love cannot truly happen or manifest until one truly recognizes and respects the Self. This all leads back to the receptive energy of which I spoke. For how can you love Self when you do not know Self? Do you know what a book is about before reading it? Take time. Take time to know yourself. You are the greatest gift to yourself. Also know that you are of Spirit, one and the same as Spirit. You have created density as a challenge to overcome, for when you overcome you will be in a lightened body. Know that you are more important than anyone you may encounter outside of yourself, as you are the co-creator in this journey. In order to love and honor another being it is necessary to honor, know and love the Self. Take time to know. So Be It.

See workbook questions for "The Feminine".

Chapter 4
GRACE
INTEGRATING GRACE, BECOMING GRACE
TRANSMITTING GRACE
By Talemahe'ke

I wish to relay to you my experience with the gracious energy patterns. It is my chosen occupation in this dimension to play with the energy of grace and impart the knowledge of such to those with profound interest.

It is essential to first know the reason why it is important to incorporate grace into one's awareness, to bring it into consciousness. It is a very delicate frequency to be practiced with the utmost of respect and gentleness. The frequency of grace is as fine as rosewater mist. It is unobservable to the physical eyes but can be felt within the heart.

Grace is a necessary component to a life of compassion. If one wants to experience love, one must first find grace. When the experience of grace envelops the person, it is an opportunity to blend with all that exists. There is no harshness in grace, no resistance. I live in the grace and move completely with the flow of energies about me. I create no resistance to spirit. Grace is necessary to move into the essence of light-being. Walk through your day filled with delicacy, find the most feminine energy possible within your being and become it. We all have feminine energy within. It is possible to present a feminine side even within the most masculine body.

I shall present to you what your world will look like when the majority of your persons accept and walk in grace. It will amaze you that a world today so filled with violence can be so peace-filled once the mass consciousness accepts grace as a valid frequency. It is evident to many soul eyes that grace will create a much lighter earth-plane dimension. Therefore some become desperate and hold onto frequencies of fear and grief, not allowing the lightness to take hold. There are many that hang on to the comfort of the density. It is a familiar frequency, that of fear. We however are choosing to play with lighter essence. That is how I reside in this fifth dimensional atmosphere. And you are quickly learning the lessons on how to reside here as well.

See workbook questions on "Understanding Energy of Grace".

INTEGRATING GRACE

My name is Talemahe'ke. I speak to you today about grace integration. There are profound aspects within the energy of grace, which tend to inhibit the traditionally third dimensional human. You may feel very resistant to the energy of grace because there are aspects of intensity of light within the element of grace, and this will essentially blow away denser energies. Some of these energies act out behaviorally in ways that you might call addictive patterns within your being. It is such that when you, as a third dimensional being (and of course all-inclusive dimensional being) become the energy of grace, you no longer can be attached in the same way to material objects or experiences. These experiences may have at one point in time created pleasure for you, or at least an escape from the denial of accepting the Self as Divine.

You will no longer experience pleasure in the same way, but will know the greatest of joy, the greatest of blissfulness. Yes, when walking in grace, when being grace, it is as if the vision changes. To be eligible to maintain a state of grace, to be the frequency of grace, it will be necessary for you to surrender your entire being. This is a very frightening aspect for human nature to accept. In the eyes of the ego self it will seem as if you will disintegrate and will no longer exist. But this is not so, dear ones. If you walk in the fifth dimensional energy spaces of grace for just a moment, you will know how profound, how blissful, these energies are. And you will want them. You will crave them much like you now crave your addictions to (so be it) your alcohol, your drugs, your material wealth, etc. You will crave that state of grace for it is so beautiful when compared to the elements of materialism and of being physical, as you have previously known it.

You will never again want to walk the earth plane without, at least, the essence of grace by your side. And eventually you will want to become the essence of grace yourself. Let me emphasize what an extreme transition it will be for you when you become the energies of grace. For when you become grace itself, you become the divine essence in physical incarnation. And you will exactly know spirit and what it is, for you are spirit. You just do not know it at times. You will also know the divine nature of your physical being. And you will honor and revere your physical, emotional, and mental bodies. You will carry these bodies with you in this state of grace. It will be a blessed union. There will also be a blessed union of each and every dualistic possibility within your third dimensional perception. You will no longer see separation as you see it prior to the integration of the graces. You will begin to fully merge your perception of male and female. You will also begin to blend the concepts of good and evil, of light and dark, right and wrong, etc. When the dualities merge, when there is no longer perception of separateness, of polarity--this will be the moment that you will understand grace and know its frequency.

Much time has elapsed in your consciousness between the start of this journey toward understanding (toward being) and your present. You have taken this time to play with the separation so that you might understand it. It is a good thing that you have done. But now you are longing to be the integration, to be the oneness. Let it be known to you that you will experience the oneness, that your consciousness will no longer struggle. It will no longer be attached to the separation. It will become one with all that is. Do not worry. Do not fret, for you will not lose the Self that you are. You will gain a Self that is much larger, much more inclusive. Also know that when you are meeting another (seemingly) separate human individual, this person is also who you are. Your consciousness is playing a game of bringing all of you to you in the physical dimension.

So it is that you sit on a chair, you create the chair to sit on only for as long as you need to physically sit. Now if it is that your consciousness is willing to move into grace, then so it will be, it shall move into grace. It shall become grace. You shall become grace. It may seem a difficult transition at first, for the fineness of grace will be foreign to the harshness that you have perceived previously. But know that the integration can be made easier by surrendering, of handing over the resistance and simply asking for assistance. You have many high beings living in physical form upon your planet earth. These beings are stabilizing the energies for the earth plane in order that the frequencies of grace and love may be brought more consistently into the earth plane.

When you walk in grace, when you become the graces, there is not much need for extensive physical activity unless it is so chosen. Your mission will become that state of grace thereby creating the possibilities for others to also become the graces. When you act, react from this place of grace, it will be quite energetically visible to others within your presence. They may turn and walk away but it also may be that they will grasp at understanding your energy patterns. I do not wish to enforce the policy of grace upon anyone but let it be known that these energies are necessary for the evolutionary growth of your planet. Your Mother Earth does know that she cannot carry the energies of grace all alone. She has given you birthplace and along with that a birthright to assist with the healing and vibratory shifts (of which you are undergoing presently) that must be transcended and integrated. Grace is a necessary component for these shifts.

Let it be known that it is my energy of grace that is the next step in your evolution. For when you "get it" and integrate the energies of grace, you will move into some of the purest love frequencies that ever have existed upon your planet. I am the keeper of the energies of grace. I hold the spaces, the energy patterns. I hold them in ways that are accessible to individual human beings. And as you read this you are asking to access the frequencies of grace. It is not necessary to have total intellectual understanding of what I have relayed to you. It is the frequencies and the way that I hold them, and the way that I shine them upon you as you read this, that are the effect.

So, let your integration process begin. And take note that perhaps in the next few days you will feel a shift, a change within your own being. You will begin to experience grace and know grace. Let it be known that there can be emotional discharge; emotional release when one is accessing finer frequencies. It is necessary to release denser frequency through the emotional and physical bodies. The mental body finds it easier to release emotions than the physical and emotional bodies.

If you release the energies of denser frequencies, you clear a path for the finer frequencies to enter. Therefore, I leave you to your integration process. And I ask you to prepare for the next step, that of transmission. It will be my duty to share with you in its totality the technology of transmission, for it is possible to give to others any frequency that you can access and integrate within yourself. So be it.

See workbook questions for ": Integrating Grace".

BECOMING GRACE

My name is Talemahe'ke. I am with you on this fine, fine day to bring you energies from my realm of existence, which is primarily a fifth dimensional consciousness space. You may join me in this space. It is my mission, my duty to be with you and teach you methods that will allow you to experience the fifth dimensional energies of grace. Grace is a necessary component for your earth plane at this time and space. As you will note, the earth plane is making a dramatic shift from one of third dimensional consciousness to that of higher consciousness. We hesitate to give it boundaries, such as to say that the earth plane is moving into a fourth dimensional space. Yes, that it is, but it is also moving into fifth dimensional spaces and beyond.

We do not want to limit the earth plane at this time, for the healing that will be necessary for your planet earth; your mother may take a dramatic leap through many realms of dimensional consciousness. We can no longer hold her to fourth dimensional consciousness. However, in order for the earth to remain in physical form it will move only as far as the fifth dimension in consciousness, where I reside. It is possible for those of you who read this manuscript to experience my energies. I expand; I extend throughout the entire fifth dimensional consciousness. I am a teacher of the element of grace. In essence then, the fifth dimension holds grace. In third dimension as humans you can understand intellectually and through a heart-felt sense the energy of grace and put it into action via transmission and service to the earth and mankind.

Therefore, it is possible for one individual to wear my energy without intellectual understanding. I can give you an experiment to play with. It is necessary for you to cleanse your mind of unnecessary clutter, so please quiet your mind. Bring your focus to the energy of your heart, the energy of love. It will be love complete that will heal your planet. And it will most necessarily be the love of your children that will heal your planet. Your children being born from this day forward will carry such intense frequencies of love that nothing will stop them. It has been that your children have experienced great amounts of abuse. Such is the way of darkness. It will be that your children being born, and yes many that are in physical incarnation at this time, will carry such light that no amount of abuse or darkness will affect their ability to love. These are children born primarily of the same soul essence. They have chosen to come into third dimensional reality with maintenance of a fifth dimensional consciousness. They will not forget much like many adults before them have.

Now go back to your heart. Feel your heart. Feel the love energy that is present. Feel the love energy of these children being born. If it is possible for you to feel love, then it is possible for you to be in a state of grace. Grace is the outer expression of love, of compassion. As I have mentioned, grace is a very delicate energy. It walks with swiftness yet remains very fine, very delicate. You may find that as you focus your heart energies on love and the expression of that love, you will move through your life more deliberately, more precisely, and yet more gently.

It will be through the state of grace that each and every individual will be moving into the knowingness, because when you walk with grace, you walk with the flow of spirit. You align what seems to be your personal will with that of a much higher Universal Will. And you do not stumble. You do not fall. You cannot fall from grace. For if you are grace, how is it that you can fall from it? It is only when you perceive an element (such as grace) as being outside of the Self that you can fall from it. But when you are firmly seated in the energies of grace, you become it.

This is the key to all of manifestation. When you become what it is that you want, that which you desire, then you have manifested it. When you become abundant in your thought, in your every expression, you are thus abundant.

It is my understanding that there may be resistance of some to move into a state of grace. But it is also my understanding that there are many that will soon be walking in a state of grace. And thus, the creation of grace will appear within your mass consciousness. Know that fear, anger, judgment will all be transcended because grace will absorb it and transmute it.

You will soon announce to and request from your angels that you wish to walk in a state of grace. Be careful to know that you are ready to walk in a state of grace, for the shift may be dramatic. You will be like me. You will be an artist and you will paint your own picture of reality in a perfect way. You will become very compassionate and will allow events to take place that previously (prior to walking in grace) you could not have allowed. You will recognize that all is divine; that each and every creation is created through the divine.

Previously, the earth plane has created struggle and strife. It is now no longer necessary to believe in such painful methods of experience. But these too were also created through the divine. Now you wish to create joy through the divine. And it shall be so, for it has been your request. It has been your contract to enter into this lifetime and experience a brief period of pain and struggle, but also experience a movement into the joy, into the bliss. You will quickly move into a state of grace, for it is not possible to close down something that has already been awakened. And it is that you want to reside with me in the graces that are.

It will be such that male and female will blend on your planet. Male bodies and female bodies will unite in a complete compassionate state of being such that a union will take place, a union not only with one another but with the God Force, the Universal Force, with the Heavens. This will be your ultimate human experience. For it is that when you unite male and female (and this I speak of male and female energies not always embodied in gender as such) the ultimate union, the ultimate human experience has taken place. And we suggest that there are many upon your planet at this time who are beginning to experience intense emotion related to the desire of this male and female union.

This union will begin to take place simultaneously all across your planet, and it will be complete. You will transcend your ego selves in this manner. It will be life force energy that will move via your passion for one another. It will no longer be blocked or stuck. It will be that you will walk in this state of grace right into that relationship that will complete the male and female union. It will be noted that the hunger for this union will stir many energies upon your planet. So it is my suggestion that you become aware of the intensity of your desire so that you do not confuse yourselves. There has been created much shame upon your planet around the areas of your sexuality. Let it be noted that most individuals carry this shame within their consciousness and thus shut down the personal awareness of these intense passions, of these intense desires to be in union with another.

It will be through grace that this shame will be transmuted as well. For there will be no shame, there will be only love. Yes it is possible for individuals to remain alone without a sexual union. It is possible. And it takes a great degree of blending within one's own consciousness to accomplish the intensity of union that can occur between two physical bodies. But this is a possible union. You can imagine yourself as having two bodies, two physical bodies. And these two bodies can unite. Your mind knows no difference between the imagined and the actual. It is all a matter of choice however.

I carry the essence of grace into your realm of consciousness so that you may pick it up and use it. It is much like walking into a room of rosewater mist. If you can imagine the gentleness of this mist and what it is like to wear this mist all over your body. You now have the physical sensation of grace. When you begin to incorporate grace within your emotional body it will be likely that your mind will interfere with the emotional body's comprehension at first. If you have not worn the element of grace prior, it will seem very foreign to your emotional body. Therefore I suggest that you play a game with your mental body, with your thought process.

You can affirm to the mind that grace has come as a helper, an assistant, and will not take over. This will appease the mind. The mind does know the element of grace, for it is part of its own creation. Perhaps you can then see in your mind's eye the frequency of grace. You can pull it in. You can reach the fifth dimension. And when you reach the fifth dimension you will see grace everywhere. Take it back with you into your third dimensional reality. Allow it then to settle into your emotional body. It will feel very generous, very warm, very loving, and very light. Walk with grace. Carry it into your relationships. You will be amazed at how easy it is to relate when relating through a state of grace. It is very easy to love from a state of grace. It is very easy to feel compassion for those you have judged or hated.

It is such a simple process. Walk in grace and all is love. When all is love, all is perfect. You may experience a desire to simply BE. There may be no need for conversation when you love through a state of grace. It is fine to be quiet, for there is enough noise upon your planet. You will also begin to only speak truth. And since truth is so very simplistic, there is not much need for words.

You may become very quiet but you will always resonate a state of grace. And thus you may find that others, those very special others will be attracted to your energy. It is such that my channel very much is attracted to my energy. And it is thus that she has chosen to wear my energy. You see, we are a very open community of spirit. We are very willing to share with you all of our energy patterns and components. We give them to you. All you must do is choose them.

I leave you today with this note: it is that I very much accept anyone and everyone into my realm of existence. All you need do is ask and I shall carry you into the consciousness of grace, and assist you in bringing that grace into your everyday existence. All you must do is say my name aloud, Talemahe'ke (Tal-uh-ma-hee-kee) and ask to have the graces bestowed upon you. Should you not feel my presence know that I am there and will be working with you regardless over time to help you prepare for and accept the grace that is yours. I send you my love and wait for your call.

See workbook pages for "More Integration of Grace".

TRANSMITTING GRACE

In order to bridge the gap between third dimension and fifth dimension, one must become accustomed to the fourth dimensional frequencies of blending. I shall discuss blending with you. On your earth plane, you cannot mix oil and water, for there is a difference in their density, in the composition of these two ingredients. They do not stay blended without additional manipulation from an outside source. If you constantly stir the oil and water they will become blended and stay blended for as long as you stir them.

We are suggesting (and I say "we" for there is much assistance in the realms beyond the third dimension) that you use a catalyst, assistance from the realms of spirit, to stir your third dimensional energies and your fifth dimensional energies. It will be as if there is another entity present to assist you with the blending.

It is not necessary to know the identity of the being that stirs frequencies. It is just necessary to know that you have assistance in this blending process. It is also necessary for you to know that as the frequencies are blending, the heavier frequencies will seem as if they are melting away. Attachments to your physical realm will become less and less. That is not to say that you will not enjoy the pleasures of physical dimension, of third dimensional reality. Oh no, for you will find even more pleasure in your 3-D world, for you will see it through fifth dimensional consciousness. You will see it as the game, as the experiment that it truly is. It will become quite a joy. For you will laugh with your creation. You will become expert creators in the physical dimension. This is your purpose, you see. It is your original intent to create.

At first when you play with these energies of grace, it may seem that you are wildly jumping out of your skin. This is simply because your skin will be taking on another form. The pigments in the skin will be changing and will seem to be glowing. You will find that your organs within the physical body will no longer need to work quite as diligently as they had in past, for they will operate more from frequencies of light. You will also understand how thought is not really the creator. Yes, it is that presently your metaphysicians understand that thought is the precursor to creation. But there is something finer, beyond thought that creates the thought.

You will discover these very fine frequencies, through grace, that create your thought, and hence then your thoughts creating your reality. It will be at this place, at very fine frequencies, that you will begin your creation. In essence all you need do is allow the graces to be a part of you, to become who you are. And your creation will become pure and perfect.

Thought is only an intermediary between the fifth dimensional frequencies and the third. In actuality no amount of trying will correct the thought. If you are trying to mend or recreate your thought from third dimensional consciousness, it will be a challenge. However, if you simply allow the graces to bestow upon you the love of spirit, creation will become its utmost finest. And then you will not need to want or desire. For then, everything on your path will be perfect creation because you see, you feel, you experience through grace. You will see shortly what I mean when I say, "become the graces." As you are reading this chapter, you are ready to experience grace in its totality.

And let me share with you that there are frequencies beyond grace that you will choose to experience. But until you become the grace of all that is, you cannot become the finer frequencies. Of course, the energies of grace seem very foreign to your third dimensional experience. Humankind has walked in density for eons and to slide directly into grace would be quite a shock to the physical being. You have become acquainted with struggle and pain and there is simply nothing painful about grace.

I suggest that you sit back and allow, simply allow the aspect of grace to take over. There is no struggle, nothing to comprehend. Truly when you become the graces you will resonate at such a fine frequency as compared to others upon your planet earth. And it will be that some will walk away, but those who are ready to experience the graces themselves will be attracted to your energies and will ask for your assistance. And it will be that as you walk in this state of grace, you will know that you are sharing this frequency with others simply by being in their presence. And when they seemingly ask for your assistance all you need do is stay present within the grace. They shall receive the energy transmission that your frequency is handing out. There is no work involved, you see. Your concepts of work in the third dimensional consciousness often become very painful and full of struggle and strife. And that is not grace at all.

You will also find yourself very much loving and feeling compassionate for all that exists. Your heart will open wide. You will become the teacher simply by acting from a state of grace. It has been a delight for me to share with you my mission. I hold the frequencies of grace so that anyone wishing to participate may simply ask and receive. Make sure that when you ask to receive the elements of grace, you are ready to receive. I leave you now in a state of grace. Blessed Be.

See workbook questions for "Becoming Grace".

Chapter 5
FAITH & RECEIVING
By Talemahe'ke

I am with you on this present day to share thoughts about faith. It is perceived from my dimensional reality that faith is a very natural element within all existence. You see, faith is a concept that only works when you have a time/space dimension within your perception. It is your perception of a split, of a separation, which causes you heartache. The heartache is taking place because of what is perceived to be a delay between emotional and thought desire, and that of the desire's manifestation in physical reality. But there must be a delay in what seems to be your time and space in order for the energy of physicality to bring into existence your desire as a manifestation. So, to appease the mind and the emotion you have created the concept of faith. And yes, faith is a wonderful thing, but I suggest that as you make your ascended trip into our fifth dimension, you leave faith behind in the third dimension. Faith is only necessary when the perception perceives a split between the now and then. When you exist in the fifth dimension, you are the now and then all at once. Yes, this is a difficult concept for your rational mind to comprehend. It is not expected to do so. But you ask about faith and how it can operate for you positively in your third dimensional reality. And this I shall explain.

So it is true that you now perceive yourself as a third dimensional being. You are doing so in order to experience all that there is to experience. You have taken creation all the way into the third dimensional realms, a very difficult task indeed. It is now time for discipline to be rewarded. We assure you that as you read this you are coming very close to a dimensional shift in your reality. But we also know in my realm that you still exist in the third dimension and you need to bring in the tools that will help you successfully complete your life in third dimensional perception. One of these tools is that of faith.

When you ask for something or want something, the only way that you can actually manifest your desire is if you continue to desire it. And definitely intention is all included. For sometimes when you desire certain things you focus on the lack of it, and inevitably create the lack of it. But this is another story, which we will discuss at later point in this reading.

The element of faith is actually a belief—a belief in yourself, a belief in the correctness of your desires. It also confirms to your Soul that you truly desire. For when you know something is right for you, for your highest good and you back it up with faith it says, "I believe." "I believe this is good for me." And it will occur. You say what you want but then there is what seems to be a time delay before its manifestation. And so you as humans use faith, faith in the knowing, to carry you through this time and space.

If it were that you could instantaneously manifest something, there would be no need for faith. And in all actuality, at times faith does inhibit you from receiving. So I suggest that you open to receiving rather than to having faith. You see, faith puts a lid on and keeps you limited more so than the energy of receiving. When you ask for something and desire something, and you open your heart, mind and body to receiving your desire, you may first get just little pieces (little indicators) of what you desire. This is because your desire's essence is coming into your field of awareness much before the actual physical manifestation of the desire. Oftentimes this delay in timing will give you a chance to grow and elevate your desires. Your expectations will change with time. Your understandings often come from the period between desiring and having. Your greatest growth can often come from such. I leave you in contemplation upon these factors that I relay to you. No longer do you need faith, but you need to receive. It is time to receive.

See workbook questions for "Transmitting Grace & The Essence of Faith" and for "Believing".

INTERACTION WITH HEAVENLY GUIDANCE

My name is Talemahe'ke. I wish to share with you a number of ways in which you may contact your own personal heavenly guidance. As workers in the Light, you know that there are energy sources or entities that exist primarily in dimensions of consciousness other than just the physical, such as I reside in the fifth dimension.

Know that these guidance sources understand what it is to be in a physical body, for they have either incarnated within the physical previously or they have had much interaction with those in physical incarnation. It is my purpose and that of many others, or shall we say ALL of the spirit beings, to assist the earth plane in this ascension process. Therefore you have designated heavenly guidance awaiting your call, awaiting your openness to their existence and their guidance.

It may be that you are attracting this guidance in your dream state. And yes, you are very receptive and open in your dream state, many of you. There are individuals however who are closed even in the dream state. But if you are researching this material, you are certainly open at least in your dream state to receiving guidance. And most likely you are open to receiving it within your day-to-day, ordinary waking consciousness.

This implies that you are aware of influences that seem very light and spirit filled. All of you have experienced what you would call a miracle of some sort. If you are experiencing a series of miracles, miraculous events, then let us say that you are "in the flow," that is, moving in the flow of your spirit path. And when this occurs it feels very good. You may also call it your Center. It is when you walk in Center that you are "in the flow."

It will be in these states that you will accept everything that exists and you will feel very joy filled. It is at this time in these states that you are very open and receptive to hearing guidance. Now, it may be that you experience auditorily the guidance from the heavenly realms. But it could be that you experience this guidance kinesthetically. Or you may see pictures or symbols. Know that it is guidance from other realms of existence, but within your field of awareness. So it is that you might call it your own, and that is fine. You need not say that you channel information from the heavenly realms. You may take ownership for the information if you wish. For we have no copyright laws in the heavenly realms.

If it helps you to differentiate the energy sources through which the information is coming, do so. It may be necessary for some to do this because it helps them to identify higher information, information that will lead to evolvement. For if you can say, "I received this information from a guide, from a heavenly source," it may prompt you to move forward with that information and that energy. There is a level of respect among much of humankind for the realms beyond the third. At some place within your consciousness, you know that you belong to all realms of existence. But because primarily you reside in third dimension you forget that you are of all creation. Therefore when guidance comes through from the fifth dimension of consciousness or others, you will honor it, perhaps more if you acknowledge the guidance source that has given you the information.

It also provides for you a very kind friendship. If you can interact with other dimensions of consciousness as friends, you will have a very rich social life. If you take any information that is of a higher nature and process analytically the meaning of this information, and integrate the information into your being, you will move more quickly forward. We are of light and we do not carry physical bodies, so we move very quickly and can advance you with our wisdom. And in the same respect we want you to share with us insights about third dimension, for it helps in our progress as well to work with all dimensions in consciousness.

As I have mentioned, it is my mission at this time and space to work with the energies of grace within the fifth dimension and share with you the graces. There are many other beings working with other types of frequencies and elements. They are very willing to share their wisdom on any such topic. So it is that you will want to access specific information from specific guidance sources. Therefore you must rid your belief system of any belief that it is not possible. For it is very definitely possible.

In order to open to your own guidance sources, you must rid your being of judgment, of skeptical statements about realms beyond your third. You know it is possible or you would not be researching this. And once you are ready, you will be led by spirit to those safe places where you can begin to, if you will, channel information. It will not happen until you are ready. This means that the walls of resistance must be knocked down. At least, much of the wall must be knocked down before you will listen.

There are many patient guidance sources in our realms. Many have been waiting for individuals to open just enough so that they can step in. And if you are already a channel for heavenly guidance, you will have the ability to influence others in knocking down their resistance. It is easy for one third-dimensional being to have compassion for another who has resistance. For you know what it is like to have resistance. Hold a space for another and use your laser energy to crumble the walls of resistance around another.

As you begin to receive information from other planes of existence, relax with it. Do not become uptight for then you put back resistance. It is not necessary that every piece of information be remembered or shared with another. In all probability, you will begin to receive information that is of a personal nature, pertaining strictly to your individual life. And as you work with this and cleanse yourself, you will find more global information coming through.

You may be given information in the form of pictures that you may paint in the physical, in the form of poetry, or the form of music or dance. Or you may be given guidance in the form of symbols, which you will interpret and share with others. And you will also be given guidance to lead you on your path toward your lifework. It will all be very pleasing. The more you treat the higher, heavenly guidance with respect and acknowledge it, the more access you will have to it.

Heavenly guidance sources will also help you integrate the information and begin to live the wisdom that is available in realms of consciousness beyond your third. So it is that I leave you now and ask you to stay tuned. And also I am asking that as you read this, if you find yourself wanting to receive heavenly guidance, then make a list of all that distracts you from moving "in the flow" of spirit, of moving on your life path. If you are running around crazily, then you have no time to receive heavenly guidance. You must quiet your mind, and your emotional body, and your physical in order to receive. It is very simple. If you constantly distract your attention from that place within yourself, you will not receive. So Be It.

INSIGHT FROM CARPATHEON
(Talemahe'ke's counterpart and soul mate in the fifth dimension.)

You allow me to speak. AH! Magnificent. You allow me to have a voice within the presence of your self. I am Carpathion (lover/companion to Talemahe'ke.) I only speak to you because you must understand the quality and intensity of love, which will soon become your experience. You have the perception that if you allow yourself to love you will not maintain and accomplish tasks, which are of an earthly nature, and in essence you are correct. You will not care. You will become evolved, involved, and accomplished beyond what you knew in third dimension.

It is my energy of strength that allows grace to recognize itself in external expression within the human nature. Strength is only accomplished within the graces by the sexual union. Strength alone withers and dies. Grace alone separates and becomes lonely. It takes strength and grace for the complete blending of the opposites, and you on your earth plane have identified grace in the feminine energies and strength in the masculine energies. We are talking about very ethereal experience. The push of the strength within the allowing of the grace becomes an incredibly orgasmic experience, as it is complete. It explodes beyond mental comprehension. You must allow it to be, allow it to exist. Allow it to work its course. For a time grace may seem to be enough, but grace cannot hold itself together in the lower dimensions without strength. In the higher dimensions strength and grace are united. You have demonstrated an over-abundance of strength on your earth plane. You have been trying to hold on with strength. You must now allow the graces to intervene and take charge. And the graces cannot take charge without the support of the strength. Until this makes sense in your comprehension within your heart, you will not understand this discourse and you will not live within the ecstatic experience which the earth planet is about to become.

It is the intention of all the energies within all dimensions that you begin to understand. It is the intention. It is also your soul's intention. Therefore you will understand and you will integrate this experience. You will feel the power of grace working within your life, within your experience. You will hug your children and your loved ones with the intent of transmitting love and grace and the task shall be completed. You need do nothing but intend and it shall be done.

See workbook questions for "Higher Guidance and Intention."

Chapter 6
UNDERSTANDING MULTI-DIMENSIONAL LIVING
By The Twelve (assisted by the Naguda Force)

There will be chaos and confusion in the lives of many within the next triennium. The minds of these individuals are being reorganized in order to accept the new fourth and eventual fifth dimensional consciousness shift. It would be helpful for light workers to work with the mental gridwork, the energy gridwork of the collective mind. It will be to the benefit of all involved if those who KNOW what is taking place begin to work to smooth out the energies of the entire planet. This only need be done during meditation and in quiet mind.

Visualize a gridwork in your mind, which might look like a grid on paper, intersecting lines with square spaces in between. Instead of the image being flat (two dimensional) imagine it to be three dimensional with planes of light going horizontal and vertical. Through this gridwork add light to the inside of the structure, first the section of the grid that is closest to yourself and thus around those individuals nearest in relationship to you. Note: is there any such person crying out to be worked with? They may not understand at a conscious level but will certainly understand and thank you at the soul level. You may also notice that there will be some that may not want you to work with their energies. You cannot manipulate someone by imposing upon his or her will. Know when to back away. Remember that you cannot harm another by working with light. If an individual is not receptive to the light at any given time, it will not enter their individual energy field.

It is imperative at this time on your planet earth that you begin to work almost daily with the energies. Do not suppose that you must go out and use physical effort to get things to move. No! This is not so. You make quite the difference by going into altered states of mind, in consciousness and playing. Literally play with the energies that you sense there. The mind does not need to be perfectly still in order to do this. That is an old way of believing--that the mind must be quiet for your work to do any good. The mind is never completely quiet, especially in the physical dimension.

You ask about ascension. How do I ascend to the finer dimensions? This is quite simple but you tend, in your physical order, to make it complicated. We are continuously taking you to these finer dimensions while you sleep. It is done with the mind. That is why we do not want your mind to be totally at rest. Imagination is the key to your success. For whatever you imagine and do not negate with thought will manifest. The reason some manifestation is delayed or halted altogether is because you create thoughts, which prevent it. Such as "I do not deserve" or "I've never been able to have this before, why should I have this now." Become aware of such thinking and transcend it, replace it with "Because I am imagining such and truly want such, I shall have such." And then let it be so. Do not dwell or obsess on such, just allow it to manifest as it will--and go about your day.

It is certainly true that you also manifest with emotion, with your heart. At this time and space, manifestations of the heart are the most accurate, the most correct. This is not to say that at a later point in your evolution you won't raise the manifestation process to a point of intellect or mind knowing. You will consciously direct thought patterns to obtain instant manifestation. But first you must know the heart level of manifestation. You have to know what is right, what is truth within the feeling center.

Humankind has already developed quite intelligent powers of manifesting with the mind. But up until this point in evolution Humankind has forgotten that the heart energy, the love energy must be included in manifesting. Therefore those who are very powerful with manifesting using mind control techniques will be prevented from their destructive powers. It will be such that those who utilize manifestation techniques from the heart energy will not be touched by those who use mind control techniques to get what their egos (not their hearts) want. This is why we tell light workers to pay close attention to what you want in your heart and manifest from this space, first from the heart and then smoothing out the thought energy around such.

Once you become expert at manifesting from the heart, you will become aware of how quickly you know whether a desire is of the heart or of the ego. The ego will not feel as intense as the heart. You will instantaneously know what is right for your highest good. At that stage, you will be able to manifest utilizing only thought waves. This will bring manifestation to you much more quickly.

We also take note that you stumble in the areas of love and relationship. Although we have presented discourse on this subject prior, we wish to explain. It will be very necessary for light workers to have harmonious relationships upon the earth plane, for to deny yourselves the pleasure of any type of relationship within the physical is truly a sin. Do not deny the Self. This is not your way to heaven. Obsessive thinking only comes out of denial. If necessary, obsess and excess until you are through. It shall not take long if you are willing to accept the joy that waits.

Take care not to be too hard upon the Self. Nurture thySelf at any given moment. Do not deprive, for there is much to be given to you. We tend to expound upon the fact that most light workers are deprivers of Self and not hoarders. You do not tend to hoard, only when you feel deprived. We see greed coming out of a sense of deprivation; therefore we digress to the point of stating once again, "DO NOT DEPRIVE YOURSELVES." You only injure the planet when you do. And if you look at the beauty of this your mother planet, you do not wish to harm her. We know this to be fact. You are all very gentle souls and love your mother dearly--for without her you would have no life. Therefore any mother truly wishes to see her children happy--truly. You must have what you deserve, most of all love. You long to have love, to feel the love that you have for so long deprived yourselves. We wish you love and pleasure for all of eternity.

One last comment: We see many of you placing judgment upon yourSelves for the sexual acts in which you participate. Know that acts of healthy sexuality are expressions (physical, emotional, mental, and spiritual expressions) of love. At least know that you can only give and receive love at the level of vibration in which you presently exist. Know that each and every individual is evolving continuously and so the one who commits acts that are seemingly not healthy to your belief, is acting only out of the vibratory field in which he or she exists at the present. Many improper, vile acts involving sexuality take place on your planet every day. These are not loving behaviors by any means, but acts of violence and control. These shameful violations are committed by those who are not in the vibration of love and ascension. Do as we say--work with the mental gridwork within your own energy field first and so move onward to work with the energy of loved ones, and then to the others of your planet. When working strictly with energy, there can be no judgment. You only judge acts of behavior, you see.

It is so that when you as individual completely merge with soul you will be complete. You will be consistent in your behavior and your personality so that you will be ready to lift off the earth plane enough that you will become an observer. You will however still be participating in that you will see the highest good at all times. You will not judge anything that takes place in action. You will utilize energy to evolve everything around you. You will certainly not speak of much except evolution. You will love. You will be love. So Be It.

See workbook questions for "Understanding Multi-Dimensional Living."

SHIFTING INTO MULTI-DIMENSIONAL PERCEPTION

It is true that the planetary changes and astrological manifestations of change can coincide with personal internal change. This does not exclude external changes, which are personal. You are right indeed to suggest that your attitude can contribute to the tensions in your life and also toward the ease or difficulty of manifesting your desires. Yet it is best, if you can, to follow the flow of experience as it happens to you. Follow flow without resistance. It may be necessary for you to become more involved with the light, more instructed by light frequency. It is important to stay grounded or as present as possible within the third dimensional reality perception. In this way fully transcend and work from a higher level of consciousness in all that you do.

Now, what we are saying is that the perception of third dimensional reality is not a truth, it is an illusion. What you have in your third dimension is only part of the whole. It is a part that you have chosen to section off and observe. But you were never to observe it from a third dimensional perception. It was intended (but of course the intention was changed) that you would play with third dimensional reality. Therefore you would have stayed within a perception of All-That-Is. We know this may be a difficult concept to understand, to absorb. It is not a concept of logic, it is as if you look through different eyes when you perceive strictly through third dimensional consciousness. You see singular pieces of reality. You see separate human beings. When perceiving through multi-dimensional eyes, yes you do see singular beings but you also see and conceptualize through eyes of totality. This is a concept of a perception place, which you shall be moving into if you so choose.

It will be necessary for those who work with light, who work with frequency and energy, to move into their multi-dimensional realities. When perceiving through multi-dimensional eyes, the third dimension becomes somewhat distant and is not quite as personal. It becomes what it was intended to become--part of the whole. It is not the most important part of the whole; it is just that you make it such. You make it as if third dimension is all that there is. This is the illusion. You spend much, much, much time pouring out energy into maintaining structures, which do not play an important role in multi-dimensional reality. You forget that you know multi-dimensional reality, because you were created from it.

We know that it is frustrating for you to intend to manifest a material item and struggle with creating it. We suggest that if you are looking at material items such as a dollar bill or that of many dollar bills...if you want to create a great sum of money, go deeper, for money is simply a third dimensional object. If however you take a look at the intrinsic reality, and the multi-dimensional reality of why you are choosing to have such wealth, you may find that at its base is the desire to maintain physical reality--a good desire if you want to continue to play the third dimensional game, through multi-dimensional reality. You need your money to exist at this time and space in your evolution. So money is necessary for survival in the third dimension.

Take a look at what gives you seeming comfort and satisfaction. Does any of it distract from your realization that you are all, that you are everything? Does your search for security distract you from your connection to the highest Self? If so, we ask that perhaps you rethink and reorganize your ideas, your beliefs about comfort and what will truly bring you pleasure. Many of your activities are third dimensional yet very spiritual, very multi-dimensional. But there are many who eat (drink, work, spend, violate etc.) only to fill themselves up and do not see this so-called pleasure as being anything other than third dimension. This is what gets you in trouble. Once you have created awareness of your multi-dimensional realities it will be more and more difficult for you to step back into addictive-type, third dimensional behavior patterns.

We suggest that it may even be difficult to spend any amount of time with individuals who do not understand this concept of multi-dimensional reality, for they may be trying to obtain pleasure in a third dimensional manner and this is only temporary joy. When you perceive through multi-dimensional eyes you may notice that when you look at your beautiful planet earth you will see colors you have never seen before. You will hear sounds that you have never heard before. It will give you great pleasure.

You are making the leap into multi-dimensional reality, but there will be times when you see only through your third dimensional eye. Do not be harsh with yourself, for you have made tremendous progress and we give much assistance to you and are very proud to be working with you to assist you in lifting the veils between third dimension and multi-dimensional reality.

We also suggest that you not get caught up in fourth dimensional reality, for there is still duality in fourth dimension. The blending is much easier in fourth dimensional reality, however. We strongly advise that you move directly into a multi-dimensional space. It can be easily done. You do not have to move up one step at a time. Or, shall we say, you do not have to move "in" one step at a time, for moving into multi-dimensional reality is an inward process. It takes place within the soul and the soul (as we are calling it--for there are many definitions) is that place within you that guides you and leads you to your most high place of being. Soul is connected with All-That-Is. And it is only through soul that you will reach the multi-dimensional reality of which we speak. It is only through soul that you find lasting pleasure, lasting joy, lasting love.

When you partake in a third dimensional activity, this activity, this experience does have an ending. It has a birth and a death. We suggest that you gladly partake in third dimensional activity but do not see it as a permanent and long lasting pleasure. Therefore if there is such an activity that you wish NOT to partake in but feel that you must, also look at it with multi-dimensional perception. Nothing is placed in front of you unless it is for your highest good in any given time and space. You are divinely guided. You sometimes forget this fact as well.

The ego would like to be at war with the soul at times. But in actuality, ego is a part of soul. It was created by soul in order to keep you in balance on this your earth plane. Ego tries to take over. You have heard of Lucifer, of your devil. Perhaps evil or Satan would not seem so frightening if you thought of the devil as that little ego self within the bigger self, within the soul self. It is only when ego becomes larger than the soul that there is evil. We do not judge that evil is wrong or bad, for darkness can only attempt to destroy third dimension. And yet there is no such element as darkness. Only light can exist in soul.

If you will, light is also a destroyer. It destroys darkness. When you bring things to light, darkness must die. That is your death. And yes, we perceive that many will choose to die a physical third dimensional death because it is much lighter, much easier to exist in the multi-dimensional reality without separating the third dimension. This is another confusing concept for you to contemplate. But do not fret if you cannot understand. Are you struggling? Do you find it difficult to manifest things that you want? Know that you can have whatever you desire, because it is all thought, neither evil nor good. You can have whatever brings you pleasure. But, if your desires are not met, the thing to do is to examine the reasons you want such things. Can they bring you pleasure in all dimensions? Will they keep you connected with soul? Will they keep you in soul? If it does not seem that they can, you may either change what you want or change the way you perceive what you want. When you begin to work with light, it becomes very difficult to manifest darkness. You can no longer manifest what will bring darkness to you. When you do, it becomes very uncomfortable. When you begin to ask for divine guidance and only work in the light, those manifestations that distract you from soul will be difficult. We are not saying that those things that you want are of darkness, but that your perception regarding those items may not be elevated enough at this time and space. We suggest then that you go very deep within and feel the multi-dimensional pleasure of those items on your want list.

When you ask for something in full knowledge of the multidimensional aspect of reality, you will bring in the highest multi-dimensional experience possible. When you truly, truly feel, that is when you shall have. There are many things that can get in the way of feeling however. First of all, as we mentioned earlier, some of those things on your want list (when you look at them through multi-dimensional perception) may no longer be necessary, may no longer be wanted when you are truly looking through a multi-dimensional eye. It may not be necessary for you to have three or four million dollars, or many material goods, and yet it may. It may not be for your highest good at this time to manifest a new relationship or new job, and yet it may. Examine your desires at deeper, more multi-dimensional levels and you will begin to see how, why and the timing of manifestations in their truest essence.

So you may scratch some items off of your list. Also it may be necessary to minimize the number of items you focus on. You have existed for quite some time in a third dimensional framework. It is difficult to learn creating something from a multi-dimensional framework. Your mind has been set up to look at each experience through a third dimensional focus. And when you shift into a multi-dimensional focus, you are using physical, emotional, mental energy to make this shift. It is a process. You may put on the top of your want list, "I want always to perceive through multi-dimensional eyes. I want to perceive through soul at all times." When you ask for this, this will become your main priority of focus. This will become number one on your want list.

The third-dimensional mind can only focus on one thing at a time. When you begin perceiving from a multi-dimensional focus, you will perceive on many different levels at one time. You will see the pasta on your plate. You will see it with third dimensional eyes and your third dimensional stomach will say "yummy, yummy." But your multi-dimensional soul reality will say "Oh! How beautifully we have created our third dimension. Oh! What aroma, what pleasure this shall bring to my soul." And it will incorporate the experience of this pasta into the whole of All-That-Is. It adds more pleasure to the All-That-Is.

So when you begin to perceive multi-dimensionally, prepare yourself for what will feel very ecstatic. It will become ecstatic experience. You will feel pleasure in the strangest things. You will no longer separate out third dimensional experience as just third dimensional experience. We sense that you need time to digest this food that we have given. Blessed Be!

TRANSMUTING FEAR

There is often great distress in your field of receptivity. We attempt to connect with your heart energy, but find it very cluttered at times, musty from the frequency which you on your earth plane consider fear. This frequency of fear is very tight. It contrasts with the frequency of what you determine as love on your planet (your identification of love, however, is quite limited.) This is the duality you see. Love versus Fear. In essence, if you were to pull these two frequencies into alignment, into one such frequency, you would come up with quite a phenomenal experience for yourselves. Yes, we are here to teach the skills needed to combine these frequencies of love and fear. You will first learn by feeling the fear within. What does it feel like? What does it do within your body? Do not be afraid of fear itself. Allow it to have a voice and ask it to help you transmute the fear into love.

Now let us look at the frequency of ecstasy as you on your earth plane might label such. Ecstasy can help you to shift from a state of fear to positioning within love. Ecstasy is a frequency that vibrates at a very rapid rate, and is also very deep (meaning its intensity is very strong.) It is so rapid that you in third dimensional reality can only handle its vibratory rate for brief, brief periods in your time and space. It is now appropriate for the human vibratory rate to change dramatically all at once. Thus a fourth dimensional, and for many, a fifth dimensional perception of reality will become very clear. In fourth dimension the consciousness begins to pull apart the third dimensional constructs and ideas. It begins to see the shadow side of reality in fourth, the "gray" areas if you will. In these gray you areas there can be found permanent truth and temporary illusions of truth which sometimes hold improper 3D forms in place on the earth plane. From fifth dimensional consciousness light can be shed upon the shadows to determine the permanency of particular forms, ideas, situations, relationships, etc. The fourth and fifth dimensional perceptions then work together within your ascended consciousness to create a more perfected manifestation in third dimension. It will be necessary for one to be present in fourth dimensional perception in order for ecstasy to maintain its stay within the human framework. Therefore we now prepare you for this next rung on the evolutionary ladder. Pack your bags!

Ecstasy, as you will envision it in the mind's eye, is a flood of colors, waves, and power. Much as you watch the flooding take place upon your earth plane, ecstasy will create a flooding in the fourth dimensional perception. It is the dominant frequency. It is the creator and the creation of all that exists in the fourth dimensional reality. Certainly, one still residing primarily in third dimensional reality will make judgment upon what occurs in fourth dimensional reality. In fourth dimensional perception, duality in subtle form is still present, but only for blending purposes. However, you, in third dimensional form cannot blend the opposites or unify the duality. It was created as such to lend opportunity for respect to each polarity as it exists. Thus until one gives unconditional respect for such opposites as male and female equally, one will be unable to maintain credence in fourth dimensional reality.

Thus until you give unconditional respect to each individual frequency of love and fear, there will be no possibility of the blending. You have been given this opportunity in fear to allow better understanding of such frequency. Often you run from such frequency and do not give it proper attention. Presently you are moving inside such frequency and examining it. This will enable you to develop respect for the purpose of the fear frequency. Acknowledge that in times of impending danger, fear will become a lifesaver. However, much of what one creates fear about in this time and space is ego exaggeration of impending doom. Know that fear based on irrelevant data is created by ego in order to maintain the status quo of existing creation. One must transcend ego manipulation in order to move into fourth dimensional reality and beyond.

See workbook questions for "Shifting into Multi-Dimensional Perception".

PHYSICAL AND EMOTIONAL RELEASE

We speak with you on the topic of release and recreating. It may seem as though you are tormented by pain, emotional pain that is created from your desire and goes deeply into the woundedness of your soul's energy pattern. The physical often carries an element of frequency remembrance. Let us explain this to you.

As you progress through lifetimes of experience, you are programmed to remember certain experiences only through the emotional body. When you live a lifetime and you have so called "negative experiences" (experiences that tend to be very destructive to the energy of spirit), you carry this conditioning, this imprinting with you into the next lifetime. And so on, and so on, until you reach a place of awareness in which you can energetically release from the physical and emotional bodies all of these so-called negative energy imprints from past experience.

Now you say, "I have negative experience in this lifetime that I must transcend." So it is true, but know that you came into this lifetime carrying an energy pattern that was created by you from your experiences of other lifetimes. And it is NOW, in this lifetime, at this time on your planet earth that all destructive energy patterns are being transcended. Therefore you are remembering all of the negative (or what you would call negative) experiences throughout time, throughout your soul time.

But remember that you do have very positive experience with which to relate. It just is that at this time there is a cleansing going on upon the earth plane. So if you are attempting to create certain experiences for yourself and these creations are not manifesting in the physical, take a good look at why you are trying to create them. And when the element of why is understood it will be much easier to redirect your desire, in a more appropriate manner.

Let us give you a scenario:

You are feeling lonely and unloved. Let us say that there is a certain individual that you wish would come into your life and love you, but this individual refuses. Know that you are playing out the karmic game with one another. It is very sad indeed that one should want and the other should not, for this is not the ideal structure within which the earth needs to mend herself. Her people are truly loving. If you attempt to bring another into your life and this other is refusing, step back and allow the graces to do the mending for you. Obviously, there are karmic tugs getting in the way of the pure love. Release the situation to spirit, to your guidance sources. Ask them to transcend the love so that you may either heal and bring together the relationship or heal within yourself in order that you may create perfect relationship with another.

If you act out of desperation, you create resistance. It is an unconscious motivation. It is like a magnet repelling. If you are in desperation your charge is too strong and you will repel the other. If you are attempting to manifest a situation in your life and things are not moving toward you, then you are also repelling the situation with your desperation.

As we have mentioned in earlier discourse, talk to your emotional body. Begin to experience your emotional body as a denser energy body than that of your mental energy body. Allow it to have its sadness but create continuous communication with it. For you can get lost in emotion.

When the physical and emotional bodies are in equal balance, you shall have peace in your emotion. Desperation, the feeling of longing, of sadness due to not having something, is caused by an imbalance in the physical and mental bodies. It is a physical craving that desires experience. Know that your physical is not your strongest asset within the whole of you. It must work with you, and also your thought patterns must work with you.

So, when you experience this craving, this longing, this physical desperation, take a good look at how your physical body is interacting with your mental body. Is the craving creating a thought, which says, "I do not have." For we have told you that "I do not have" creates more of the "I do not have." Take a very good look at the physical dimension of things and ask that spirit connect your physical and integrate it into spirit so you will know that your physical body is indeed a spiritual body.

Concentrate on raising your vibration, your vibratory rate. If you lie very still, you can feel the vibration of your body and you can elevate it, minimally at first, and eventually at very accelerated rates. You will consciously create a vibratory shift. When you concentrate only on vibration, your longing and your desires are transcended. Your thoughts are transcended and transformed. And your physical body can release old patterns.

Know that you might be creating from old patterns, old vibratory spaces. Therefore, in order to change the rate at which you manifest, know that the rate of change will happen much more quickly if you focus only on increasing your vibration and doing the light work.

We find that you talk too much on your earth plane. You spend too much time explaining things and telling things when you should be doing things. You should be elevating your vibratory rate by whatever means you enjoy. If you do it in meditation, so be it. If you do it during your job or your yoga class, so be it. But concentrate only on elevating your physical vibratory rate. If you work at the densest places (that of the third dimensional physical vibration) you elevate them and push them along with the emotional vibration and mental vibration into fourth, fifth and beyond. It is your physical that is slowing you down. So it is necessary to work on the physical body as well as your auric bodies and your light bodies. Make sure that you do not forget the physical that is creating the longing.

In all actuality, your longings for manifestation are simply your physical body longing to be reunited with spirit. And it cannot do so if your vibratory rate is too slow. You must constantly elevate your vibration. That is all for now.

PRESERVING PHYSICAL HEALTH
The Twelve & Naguda Force

We are The Twelve with the assistance of the Naguda Force. You are at a time in evolution in which the energies of earth are being greatly stirred. We suggest that for your next twenty years, your physical bodies will be adjusting to the new energies coming from Universal Flow and being integrated into your consciousness.

Your so called Ozone Layer has holes and gaps in it. This is good for it allows the energies beyond your third dimensional consciousness to enter. If you want to ascend, you will need to move out of your third dimensional awareness because a shield of gravity has been placed around the earth planet. This was to keep you in density. When this opens up you receive more radiation, so you will no longer stay as dense.

We assure you that as this shift is taking place, in the interim, until you know full well your multi-dimensional consciousness, the physical aspect of the self may resist with disease and dysfunction. We do have remedies that can assist you as you are in this interim stage between third dimensional awareness and that of your most high dimensions.

Most importantly, let us emphasize the fact that your physical body is a very gentle, fragile form when used improperly. Of course its strength and agility can be improved. Your physical body is a very vulnerable aspect of your wholeness. Therefore you must take care of it with spirit. As you become aware of your multi-dimensional self, it may seem that your physical body is quite sluggish and it may be hard to move. Third dimension does move quite slowly as compared to your higher dimensional realities. But take heed in knowing this and take care of your body. In particular, there will be a time when you will have periods of fatigue, of being tired, alternating with periods of quite elevated energy.

We suggest that the best way to work with this alternating energy is to follow it. There may be some of you working on the inner planes that may need more rest than others. And we suggest that you honor your physical body's requests for sleep, for nourishment, for pampering. For the body is your most essential resource at this time.

What you are learning in this process is how to elevate your frequency in the physical body. It will be quite a profound revelation for you. Therefore, you are going to need to take your physical body along on this ascension, for that is the full enlightenment. Know that your physical body is just as divine as any other part of you. You created your physical body from your own divinity. Remember that you chose each and every aspect of your being. Therefore it is your responsibility to care for your physical body when it calls out to you. It is very easy to neglect the physical aspects of Self because they are slow moving, seemingly so but not in actuality. In actuality they are moving right along with the rest of you.

We shall now suggest an exercise that you may do to encourage your awareness of the physical body as divine energy. We suggest that you sit in your nudity. If you are not comfortable nude, perhaps wearing as little clothing as possible during this exercise would be good. Begin by touching your toes. Begin by feeling the cracks and crevices, indentations of the skin. Follow all the way up your foot, and ankle and leg. Begin to know your physical body in the way that many of you have begun to know the emotional body, and the intellectual body. Oftentimes you spend many, many hours examining your mental process and your emotional process but forget that your physical body has much wondrous elements about it.

You may find moles, creases, things you never knew were there. Continue all the way up your body, feeling it with your hands, exploring it with your eyes, smelling it with your nose. It is much like making love to yourself. When you have a partner, oftentimes during lovemaking you kiss, you touch; you caress every place upon that partner's body. It is exciting. But it is also that you know your partner's body better than you know your own. Perhaps you have bumps, bruises or sore spots upon your body that you were too busy to recognize previously. Nurture those areas that need extra loving care. For your body is your best definition at this time of what it is that needs to change. If you are physically ill, take heed not to punish yourself further by analyzing what you have done wrong. Take advantage of your illness to relate to your physical body. Take the time out to get to know your physical body even further.

There are sensations to the physical body that feel very wonderful. We suggest that you continue to excite the physical body with these physical sensations, but remember that your physical body is connected to all different realms of your experience. When you engage the physical body in an experience of excitement, remember your divinity and that, what pleases the physical dimension also pleases many other dimensions. If you keep this awareness in the forefront of your knowing, you will do well. If you pursue physical pleasure only without multi-dimensional awareness it will be difficult to maintain.

See workbook questions for "Physical and Emotional Well Being".

RELEASING AND UTILIZING PSYCHIC INFLUENCES

Many of the challenges that you experience in your third dimensional earth plane reality can be attributed to the influence of psychic forces. As you realize your existence, your purpose as a light worker on the planet earth, you will experience momentary glitches along the path. You might say that primarily you have exhausted and released most of your karmic influences; influences from past that remain in your memory patterns. You may have released the majority of those, but still you experience resistance in your creation. This could be caused by the influence of another person through the psychic plane. Let us explain.

There is a stratum, a layer of consciousness, which allows you the ability to telekinetically transport your thought to another. This is a very thin layer of consciousness, which exists between fifth and sixth dimensions of consciousness. There are many who are and have been very skilled at using this stratum for their own advantage. It is not necessarily an evil thing that a person might manipulate another through this stratum. It is your judgment placed upon their deeds that makes it appear evil. It is true that as you fill with light, your manipulation of another will only be for the highest good. And it is true that there have been many who have used and manipulated another in essence NOT for the highest of good purpose or intent.

You are being manipulated and used in this manner all the time, unless you become aware of this stratum, unless you become aware of those influences upon you. This will take extreme concentration and awareness. Our suggestion at this point in your time and space is that you spend much time in your meditative state in order to become clear about what influences you. All light workers will find themselves alone for periods of time while they meditate.

It is only through awareness that you can release the psychic hold of another upon you. Many people in this your time and space are utilizing this stratum to influence others, but they are unaware that they are doing so. They have spent other lifetimes developing their talent for using this stratum and perhaps using it intentionally NOT for the highest good. And as they permeate this lifetime, they bring along with them the tools (on an unconscious level) necessary for utilizing this stratum for influence. It is very important as you fill with light to become conscious of all your creation. You will know when it is for the highest good and when it is not. And the more light filled your life and your energy bodies are, the easier it will be to influence and manifest through this stratum. It may even be possible for great works to come about without lifting a finger.

Before you begin to utilize the stratum of the psyche to influence, you will want to release those influences upon yourself. You will need to go into your meditative state and in your mind's eye you will visualize this stratum. You may feel physically non-existent when you touch upon this stratum. All that exists in this stratum is the energy of thought. Visualize this stratum as energy and remember that it is very thin, but it has very much power. Visualize the stratum around your physical, emotional, mental, auric and light bodies. It exists as a plane within all bodies. That is why it has so much power.

As you look in on this stratum, you will see streams of energy that are denser than other areas within the stratum. And these streams of energy move from this stratum into your physical, emotional, and mental bodies. Think of balloons with a string. These are pockets of energy, which another has placed in the stratum. They have streams of energy, which are tied directly to you, and the other person is pulling on another string attached to the same pocket of energy. It is as if you were a puppet. They pull. You react. It is in the psyche, within the psychic realm, that we control one another. All you must do is invent a way of releasing these strings of energy from your person. It may be that you invent a huge pair of scissors and you cut the strings so that they no longer touch you.

If you will notice, many of the streams of energy end up right in your solar plexus, your power center, in other words the center of reaction. You may cut the strings. You may light an imaginary match and burn them. It would probably be best though, if before you do so you climb the stream of energy, put yourself in this pocket within the psychic stratum, and send a message to that other individual telling him or her that you are now releasing yourself from this bind. It would be the kindest thing to do. Now, this is all done during meditation. You do nothing on the physical level with the situation at this time. If you were first to explain in person what you were doing, the other person might unconsciously create another pocket of energy with streams controlling you. So it is that in your mind's eye, you climb to the psychic stratum and send a message that yes you are releasing this other person's hold on you. Send them love and tell them that you forgive them. Come back and do your releasing.

Then, you can go onto the next pocket of energy and the next person, and release that one. The psychic stratum, the energy within the psychic stratum is very malleable. It can be reworked very easily. So if you are in a hurry to do your release work, you may go in and visualize yourself as combining all the pockets of energy into one big pocket. And when you have done this, you can send healing, love and forgiveness to all and every one who has ever had any psychic influence over you whatsoever, for all lifetimes. And then you can do one major release. You really need not know who it is and what it is that is controlling you. All you need to do is release.

After you feel cleansed through this meditation, you may want to reenergize your physical and emotional bodies by doing some physical release work, some bodywork, and some emotional cleansing. Your physical body, your emotional body and your personality may feel very attached to being controlled. It will simply be a matter of washing all remnants clean. And once you are cleansed, you will take a good look at your life and what it is that you want to manifest for the highest good. If you are having difficulty in getting the assistance of another to manifest for the highest good, then you may utilize the psychic stratum. We shall explain how to do this in your meditative state.

You will go into the psychic stratum just as you had before. You will pull in streams of energy. It is just like baking a cake. You know that you need certain ingredients to make it work. Therefore, in the psychic stratum you will find frequencies that are somewhat different than frequencies in other dimensions of consciousness. They are used specifically for telecommunication. Therefore they are different looking and different feeling in their nature.

You may pull three, four, five, six, maybe hundreds, maybe thousands of frequencies into this pocket you are creating. It can be quite fun. It can be like making mud balls as a child. Therefore you can pull from any area within the psyche, frequencies which will work for you in getting positive reaction from another. Once you have completed your pocket and it is vibrating at a very high rate (now remember you are creating with light, so you want only the lightest of frequencies), you will send a stream of energy down to the other individual or individuals that will be assisting you on your journey.

Be aware that if you are sending energy to another, the stream may move a bit or it may break apart and shine its light to three or four individuals. Or it may shift completely from the individual that you thought you wanted this assistance from, to another. Once you have sent the stream, you will also carry a stream from this pocket with you back into your physical, emotional, mental, auric, and light bodies. You are holding this but be aware that you bring this stream through the channel of light that goes to your soul into the *Monad* (the One—the highest level in consciousness that a person can reach through basic meditation and consciousness). Make certain that this stream comes directly through and into your heart center. If you wish to ground the stream into the earth it will have more stability. Now you have made a direct telecommunicative link to another. You will be able to, at this time, send thought and influence through this stream of energy.

However, we suggest that before sending you meditate on the thought of doing so. You will want to be certain that your thought is creating highly and not of density. You can use the psychic strata to manipulate and influence others, but also you can use it to influence your animal kingdom and your plant kingdom. It may sometimes be utilized to influence your material world as well. It is difficult to manipulate your material, physical world without compassion for the object you are influencing. It is true that your material world does have some influence of feeling within it. This is a very new concept to many on the earth plane, for you did not previously know that the woods, metals, rocks, etc. have remnants of feeling within. They come from the earth and the earth carries emotion.

Therefore, in order to influence your physical environment, you must treat it with respect and compassion. If you have items in your possession that you no longer care about, give them to another who will care for them. If you are attempting to create something material in your life, you must feel very compassionate about that particular object. It will become much more evident for those of you doing light work that the only way creation will take place is if it comes directly from your heart.

There are two ways of manifesting. One is with heart energy and one is with low-level desire (creating from areas of the first three charkas and the power centers.) However, without love, it is not pure creation. You will not create purely without love. And it becomes very painful for light workers to have creation within their existence that they do not love compassionately. That is all.

THE CLEANSING OF THE PSYCHE

You, dear ones, are currently cleansing your mental precognitions of reality. We assure you that the grieving that you choose to experience is only necessary because you so choose to be in grief! This is another so-called illusion. Do you understand that the healing will not take place just because you do your mental homework? Oh no, it will only leave your condition if you choose to let it go from your physical body as well as from your emotional body.

If you choose to remain in physical form, we suggest that you move into nature as much as possible. Be with the forces, which create essence. Do not place emphasis on relationship outside of self at this time. It is important for many who seek this dimensional shift to focus only on Self and the clearing of the psyche. The psychic consciousness at this your evolutionary time and space is filled with clutter from an undeterminable amount of energies. Not only has mass human consciousness filled the home space of the psyche with clutter, so too have the creational energies of all time and space left remnants of its work there. In order for the shift to occur, the psychic energy fields must be cleared of webbed, tangled and matted energy. This is where the force of entropy comes in. We are suggesting that you learn to work the forces of energy on a personal level first, so that the energies can then be reformatted at the Universal level.

It is part of your experiment you see to remain in physical reality, so you must learn to keep the outer structure intact while reorganizing (literally blasting away the old organization) the inward structure. Once the inward structure has been reformatted, the outer manifestation will follow suit. This is a Universal Law. Whatever shall change within must change without. It is not necessarily so that whatever changes without will change within. You make many changes to the outside walls of your homes and building structures but this does not necessarily change the energy within the building. It only creates appearance. You must do the work necessary to change the internal pieces of the psyche.

We honor and assist in this time of great transition for you and others who truly desire change. It is of the greatest mission that we work together to climax into the heavenly realms of existence. Blessed Be.

SELF LOVE

To be certain of your heritage here upon this planet earth, you must perceive visions of a home state of being. Rest gently within your heart in order to be kind to yourself. You must feel somewhat nurtured in this time of tumultuous events upon the planet. Love! That is the frequency that will open the heart and inevitably heal the planet. Love is your only answer.

We give advice based only upon the cries of those who seek what you would term enlightenment. Only those who seek shall find. Open your hearts and your genitals to love, the truth that love exists. We know that you have many such frequencies disguised as love upon your planet. These are frequencies that allow manipulation of another. They vibrate at a very low rate of speed, attempting to corral the frequencies of those who are confused and unsure. This is your chance (those of you who question) to come into a frequency of love and thus heal yourself. We serve you in this way, only with love. We respect your perseverance in this attempt to become free of manipulation. We say that your chance is now. Renounce everything that controls your frequency, everything that disbars you. If you must, make a list and eliminate one by one those that serve you not. This is urgent. We insist, only care for yourself at first. Later you can care for those whom you love. If two of you shall come together in love and respect, so too shall you have complete joy and forgive past hurt and resentment.

It will be said from our perspective that many of you hang onto old worn-out items, which must be discarded in order that you may take on the new. We speak of relationships as well as material goods. We know that many of you substitute the material for what you do not obtain through your chosen relationships. So be it, but we caution you. There will be much disturbance in the material plane to get your so-called attention. We wish for you eternal happiness, and know that material items will not provide such, for they are temporal. We urge you to search for true purpose of heart; for it is time that each contributes in this way to the earth plane.

We insist that you first take time and space to nurture your Soul energy. Look inside. Find that which truly makes you happy and GO FOR IT. There will be nothing to stop you from having what you want except your own doubt and fear. This you can quickly transcend. We wish you well for these days ahead. For this time shall bring solidity to that which pleases you. The Heavens are Blessing you.

CHANGING BELIEF PATTERNS

The human condition as you perceive it at times can be very heavy, very dense. As we have stated before, this perception comes from the belief that you are separate. Thus we want to expound upon belief patterns, and how to change them quickly.

First of all, we ask that you make a commitment to this change. Honor yourself enough to say, "I willingly commit to changing any belief structures which get in the way of my growth, my evolution." If you make this statement to yourself and the Universe, you have accomplished the primary step. Next, begin to feel within your emotional body the heaviness of negative beliefs. Take a look at what you have created with heavy beliefs. It is as though you cannot lift your feet off the ground when you play the game of negativity. Yes, it is a game, for you can change the rules if you so choose.

We next suggest that you discard events or situations that will throw you back into the spaces of heaviness. If you want to believe that life is beautiful and you can have it all, why would you continue to spend hours of your time with persons who continue to believe that life is miserable? Take a good look at this belief system. Make an effort to pull away from these people at least until you can get your head clear. If necessary, become your only friend for a while. We know this advice scares many people, for it may mean a complete transformation of lifestyle. That is why we ask for commitment upfront. And a total commitment it must be. Won't it feel better to live a positive, light filled life rather than heaviness and negativity? It is possible, you know. And it is the only way to ascension.

Christ did not ascend while believing that life on planet earth or anywhere was not good. In fact, Christ had no belief structure. For when you are truly ascended there is no need for beliefs, there is only love. This is difficult for you to understand, but as you ascend you begin to let go of all belief, for there truly is only knowledge. Truth is all there is and the physical plane (as in third dimensional perception) does not exist. You will no longer see the physical realm as a separate realm. If it were all-inclusive, why would you need belief structures? Only to keep it separate, you see.

For now, however, you do carry around a belief structure that must be reorganized as the first step toward enlightenment. We know that many humans carry opinion about issues, about the way things should be. Take a good look at your opinions, for some of these will be the first to be discarded. You will have fewer opinions. You may prefer to eat Italian food rather than Chinese at any given time, but this is just a preference, not an opinion. Do you understand?

The next step in the game is to allow flow to take you where it needs to. Flow is the essence of spirit in movement. Do what FEELS right and allow whatever comes into your life to be there. If there is something that does not FEEL right in your life, take a good look at what it is and ask for guidance as to how to change whatever it is. There will be immediate signals of what to do if you are receptive to the guidance that is available. Take heed not to slip back into old patterning. It will be easy to react in old ways when you first begin this process, but soon you will find yourself repulsed at some of the old ways that you had. You will find it more difficult to hang on and some patterns will be shattered if you hang on too long.

We bless you and will let you sit with this information for a while in order that you will truly integrate and allow.

See workbook questions for "Psychic Health".

BUILDING A VISION/BECOMING LIGHT

We guide you today in this instruction on how you, as a Master on your earth plane, will build your vision. Creation is so very simple, yet the human complexity within the mind has created distress and entanglement.

Humankind has broken down the elements of creation to such a degree that you must walk one step at a time. But spirit knows that this is not necessary. Spirit knows that you can soar above your planet. But it is as if human nature wants proof. "Prove it to me!" And so you must take one step at a time. This is due to your insistence on having proof.

You can blend your physical body into your so-called auric body and it will be blessed with much lightness, many pleasantries, and much freeness. As it is, where you are at presently, you feel not free. You feel much boggled down. This is the irony within your human perception. You listen to your birds on one side and your carpenters on another. Now who is freer? It is that the birds live without mansions. They live within themselves. They need no houses. They need no shelter because they are sheltered from within.

You need your automobile to travel from one place to another while your bird takes off in flight on its own. The bird has no awareness, has no consciousness in the way that a human has consciousness. So that is your advantage. You do have consciousness. If you blend the assets of the bird with the assets of humankind, you would have it all. Therefore it is to your advantage to learn from your birds, your winged creatures.

Let us begin with an explanation of how you as human may soar. As you work with your frequencies and you work with your light, and you begin to elevate your vibration, your physical body will begin to dissolve. It will begin to disappear from the physical vision. It will still be visible when you direct it to do so, but you will have the ability, at will, to move into such a light body that seems quite impossible at this time.

There is an space that you may move into at will. This place in consciousness is found through the process of meditation. It is a place where you essentially can forget that you are physical in nature. And we are suggesting that in your near future you will remain in what is seemingly a meditative state for long periods of time. You will be aware of being in your light body without the seeming presence of your physical body.

Therefore, it is wise that you do your meditation in private quarters, for you may disappear and it may seem quite strange to an observer who has third dimensional perception.

We suggest that you are elevating your vibration quite rapidly because your earth plane, Mother Earth herself, is shifting her vibration. In order that you may remain on the planet, you and everyone else on the planet must elevate frequencies. Some more than others, but everyone will do so. And those who choose not to do so will leave the earth plane for less frequent places.

Do not forget that you are a spirit being and your spirit being can and will take over your physical being. It is time when you give it over. When your emotional nature no longer controls you and you no longer are consumed by heavy, dense emotions (no longer consumed by the mind and its negativity) you will then evolve and move into your light body.

We ask that you do an experiment today. Sit in your chair and begin to meditate. Begin to visualize your body dissolving, your physical body no longer existing. Exist in this mindless state for a period of time and begin to move out of your chair while maintaining this state of mindlessness. Can you do it? Perhaps not at first, but more and more you will become accustomed to not sensing your physical nature. More and more you will elevate your frequency to this state of nothingness within your mind, this state of ecstatic experience. Then you will essentially be gone from the third dimensional realm. However, it may take a period of time as you do the exercises within this manuscript, to do the clearing and shedding of old behavior patterns, thought patterns that keep you grounded in third dimensional perception. It may take some time but continue to play with these. Find the ones that you like and use them over and over again until you no longer need them.

We shall challenge you with this insistence upon your growth. For we know that the earth plane must move forward in an elevated fashion. It is essential. And if you do not do the growth work at this present space and time, you will inevitably have to do it. It is your choice for a while but only a while, for you made a choice to do this work long, long ago. So to take action on that choice now and to be diligent in your work, in your evolution is quite respectable. That is all.

GIFT OF PROPHECY

To begin this journey into the ecstasies of the other dimensions, we must ask that you begin by relaxing into the energy of peace. It is in peace that you will find everything you need. There essentially is no beginning or no end. There just IS.

Let it be known within your consciousness that there are many individualized expressions of soul that do not understand or want to understand the spiritual path. You play with fire when you begin to influence others. Yes, we say you play with fire, essentially because you will encounter angry individuals who, due to ego manipulation, do not want to see the higher path. We tell you this today because we see that there are many upon the planet that have such gift of prophecy, the gift of knowing. Yes we say there are many who have such a gift, but there are many who choose not to reveal their gifts for fear of being ridiculed. And thus there are very few who will have the courage to share the insights that they perceive as truth.

We advise that you as prophet enforce your perceptions, but do it ever so gently. Do not manipulate or persuade others that they must believe what you say. Just state your prophecy and let go. Allow the choice to be made. We know that it is frustrating to see events, circumstances about another's life and have them refuse to believe, and then watching the event unfold. It is often the element of surprise that intrigues people. Therefore when they know what is about to take place, it angers them for then they cannot be surprised. If you know intuitively of a future event, or become aware of suppressed thought or emotion, then it is easier to prepare and life will flow smoothly.

If you begin to allow this gift of prophecy to surface and use it wisely, it will create more gifts for you. An abundant flow of energy will be available for you to work with when you prophesize, when you tell the truth. We do not wish to explain at this time and space how those who are unaware of this gift can achieve it. For it will only appear when enough cleansing of the personality has taken place. It is only meant for those who will use it wisely.

Granted, there have been some who have acquired the use of prophecy and have used it in deceitful and manipulative ways, but the time of Black Magic is quickly coming to an end. For there are many light workers upon the planet who are in essence saving the planet. You, the reader, are one of these light workers or you would not be reading this work.

We close this discourse with the cooperation of our channel in slight prayer. We ask that when each of you turn your attention to the power of creation, that you attain a state of great reverence. We ask our channel to resonate this state of reverence through her work on this book so that each and every reader will read only purity, only truth. May you take these words and use them to perform your most high purpose upon the planet. We feel reverence toward you and the work that you do, for you have chosen a most difficult time in the evolution of humankind to incarnate. Thus the rewards will be great. We understand that there is much to maintain in the human form. You have emotion, thought, and physical form. You encounter and must work with many forces. We truly honor you and hope that you will honor our part (as spirit energy) in assisting evolution as well.

See workbook questions for "Creating Utopia
".

Chapter 7
MIND, THOUGHT, AND ENERGY: ITS CONSTRUCT AND PURPOSE
The Twelve assisting The Naguda Force

Please speak to us about linearity (linear thought) and how it can be most efficiently used in this our current time.

Linear motion as you know it exists only in the mental framework of the divided Self. You are part of a much larger whole but have chosen to divide yourSelves off into what is perceived as separate individual complexes of the All-That-Is. However, this is not the perception from much higher vibratory spaces.

We anticipate from the realms of higher consciousness that your third dimensional experiment will soon complete a cycle of density that became so enmeshed in the polarized negative aspect of frequency that something must give. There will be an explosion into light, the most high of frequencies that can be experienced within a third and fourth dimensional consciousness. Within the third and fourth dimensional consciousness there must be a way of "making sense" of what is happening to you. Thus the mental framework of linearity is created. In order to structure your third dimensional reality, you must maintain a degree of linearity. The details must be in place. It is, however, not necessary to keep the same definition of linear thought. The linear mental structure of the planet is quickly transforming in order that destruction does not ensue (this is due to imbalance of the mental power over other powers, i.e. emotional, physical, and spiritual power within density).

We will discuss how this change will take place, the effects upon the human race, and what the structure of rational/linear mind will look like. It has been chosen by each of you to manifest in this lifetime in order to support the evolutionary shift. It is a planned destiny that the earth plane makes this shift. If you are at all curious about the progress of this transformation, you will become "hooked" and be carried along on frequencies that will take you to places unbelievable at this your time and space within your belief structure.

We have determined just cause for this shift--it is strictly the plan. Next, we must discourse upon how the mental structure will shift. Many of you may already be experiencing headaches, dizziness, feverishness, and stiffness within upper body joints and memory loss (it is not necessary in this framework to remember consciously all that one used to remember.) These mental and physical symptoms are indications that the way you used to process thought is no longer working for you and your body is indicating this when you attempt to think in such manner. The best advice we can give at this time is to surrender to flow. Take care to know that all is divinely guided and the Universal forces will not let you fall. The best solution to all of this is to play, literally play, with Light, the finest frequency possible at this your time and space.

We suggest using guided meditation and *light techniques* (visualization methods using light to change experience—some are given later in this book) for growth. At first it will seem like trickery to the ego, and the ego will try to step in with doubt and guilt to keep its place in this our third dimensional experiment. We advise that you begin to see within your mind's eye the gridwork that surrounds each and every one of you and the planet. The gridwork has been created by the mind to keep a mental structure of light. The gridwork at one time and space was very tightly woven around the earth plane. For some of you it was too tight and created a suffocation of spirit. You essentially lost sight and connection with your soul energy. Well, my friends, the gridwork is loosening, it is becoming much more expansive and you can once again breathe the Spirit Breath. Isn't it wonderful to be able to trust that you do not have to do all the work as just a physical and mental being? You are more, so much more. And the experiment has only begun. Play darlings, Play with your creative minds. It is being given to you in order that you will remember who you really are--remarkable expressions of the God Force. There is so much Love and Creativity to be experienced by all--we cannot express to you how much for you would not believe. All you have to do is open to the Light and Love of Spirit. It is that simple. We wish you well in these days of light ahead of you.

Know that the only reason that you struggle is because you choose to hang on to the old ways of believing. Do not judge Self if this is what you are choosing, for you are learning very important lessons by hanging on. These lessons can also be learned through joy. We encourage each to take a look at how much joy can be experienced within the old linear framework?

We are not suggesting that you no longer use linearity. Oh no, it will not be possible to function in your realm without it. But the form of linear thought is changing. A much more open structure is being created. This is so that finer frequencies of spirit can begin to filter through. Together we will create heaven on earth.

It is also truth that in your physical dimension you will open the center to your heart, to that feeling place that carries much depth, much intensity. It will be necessary to feel once again. The feeling center will be your indicator of what is higher truth for you as an individual, and for what is right for evolution as a whole. Do not give much linear thought to something that is right within the feeling specter of Self. When there is indication that something is right, go with it, trust it, and then bring the process of linear thought into the picture. Use linear thought to assist in the building process. But trust the inner guidance that will be becoming a much larger part of your consciousness. You cannot build a house without a plan, but you can trust spirit to provide the plan. We bless you and will send you much guidance in these days ahead.

LAYERS IN CONSCIOUSNESS

Good Day! We join you this fine, fine morning (or whatever time of day it might be) to explain to you aspects of the conscious material within which you have been working. We have done a blending on this day. We have blended the guidance sources of your Pleiadian Brothers, (your knowledge source for love and compassion) with that of The Twelve consciousness. We do this so that an explanation of layers of consciousness can be presented with most respect and an emotional component that will intrigue you into understanding the complexities of your own being.

We begin by explaining the layer of third dimension. The third is a very misunderstood layer of consciousness. And when we say layer, we explain it as such; imagine a round ball of consciousness. And this ball may seem to exist on its own, but it is only illusionary. Imagine the ball and imagine, for now, that the ball of consciousness has a very thick shell around it. And from inside this third dimension, from inside this ball, you cannot see beyond, for it has thick outer coating that you have created. And from inside it is not easy to access the layers surrounding this third dimension, for it would seem that you are trapped inside this shell. Therefore you focus your attention only within that sphere, that third dimensional sphere.

And know you that it was this third dimensional consciousness that created this outer shell in order to experience third dimension from third dimension only. And it is in the destined creation that layers of consciousness from outside the third dimensional sphere have begun to penetrate this hard shell. It is much like you have painted the shell, and the paint is peeling. So there are holes and gaps in this shell and many of you are beginning to glimpse the layers of consciousness beyond the third. This is fun. But you are also very good at pretending that the shell still exists in its totality and it does not. It is peeling away very quickly.

We advise that you surrender to the destiny that you have created. All layers of consciousness penetrate all other layers. When awareness is present, you will KNOW that. And when you begin to recognize your awareness of other layers of consciousness, you will experience flashbacks to earlier experiences with the totality of being multi-dimensional. This is when you will begin to see your physical body as not being solid. You may begin to see gaps and holes in your body when you view it from a multi-dimensional perspective. Do not allow the fear to overcome you, however, when you begin to see these gaps and holes. We wish that this be a delightful process for you. Therefore we assist you in reformatting your thought structures around such phenomena.

It will be that when the outer shell of your third dimensional perspective begins to peel away, or fall apart, you will begin to experience other realms of consciousness. And most likely you will begin to experience some of the fourth dimensional experiences, that of your astral realm of consciousness. This is a delightful place to play, for there is still awareness of duality in fourth dimensional consciousness. Yet there is no solidity, the density that you play with in third dimension. Therefore it is easy to blend the dualities, the polarity.

Say for instance in your physical dimension, it takes a male body and a female body (or two bodies of same gender) to blend and merge on the physical dimension that can be blended on other dimensions without contact. In fourth dimensional consciousness, it is possible to merge completely the individual bodies. The merger creates tension in the third dimensional realm. So know that when you begin to experience fourth dimensional perception (and this begins by noticing a blending of all aspects of your being) the physical aspect of your third dimension will become perhaps anxiety ridden and irritated. There is still an aspect of the self that thinks it is separate. It will be good for you to ingest the idea that you can be separate whenever you please and you can be blended whenever you please. And you are the decision-maker in that process.

Now we take you to the fifth dimension of consciousness. It is in fifth dimension that you still carry an awareness of choice. You simply have choice to do as you please, but you carry no individual bodies. You embellish and are every frequency that exists within this Universal sphere of consciousness. And you have choice. You are simply choice.

In the sixth dimension of consciousness, the aspect of choice travels along into a much greater flow. It is here that you blend your will with that of the Higher Will. It is out of this dimension that you begin creation in its most perfect form.

When we move into the seventh and eighth dimension of consciousness, everything merges. You no longer see any separateness in frequency or choice. These are the dimensions of void consciousness, a place to relax and let go of stress because the nothingness sensation here will absorb and transmute all of it.

We may take you beyond the eight dimension of consciousness only in a state of receptivity. It is at moments when you have no awareness of being conscious that you move into your ninth, tenth, eleventh and twelfth realms of consciousness. The ninth layer is the layer of consciousness that allows. It is the Allower.

In your tenth layer of consciousness, there is no more. And there is an eleventh and a twelfth of which you can have perception, but at this time cannot express. These are very expansive layers of consciousness for a third dimensional being to comprehend.

You ask, "From which layer of consciousness does love come from?" When you play in realms of ninth, tenth, eleventh, and twelfth, the concept of love becomes irrelevant. For there is nothing to love, and love is nothing. Therefore we suggest that if you are playing with manifesting love within your heart, within your being, take it into your eighth and the borderline of the ninth dimension of consciousness. Allow some higher consciousness of the nothing to come in to play with the love and it will expand. It will expand!

You will notice how harsh you have been with your Selves. And love in this expanded state will bring up some disbelief and some sadness related to the way you have been treated. Therefore expect that you will need great amounts of forgiveness, which you will find comes easily as love expands. It is with this that we will disband our union, The Twelve and The Pleiadian Brothers, so that we may go and explore different aspects of consciousness.

We bid you good day and allow you to carry our frequencies with us throughout this day. And of course you may at any time carry our frequency but we give you permission on this day so that you will feel more grateful in taking it with you. Good Day!

See workbook questions for "Linearity and Layers in Consciousness".

ON IMAGINATION

There is a force that propels the so-called mind entity of the Self. This force is the imagination It is the so-called gelatin between matter and non-matter. This force will be present in all states of existence that create materialism. .

Please regard the imagination as the highest force within the mindset. Yet, on the planet earth and especially in Western Society, imagination has been regarded as foolish, as a waste of time. Now we propose that all of the resistant programming toward eliminating the fantasy world, the daydream, the imagination, be eliminated itself.

Suppose your master geniuses chose not to allow their imaginations to run rampant. Where would your technology be today? It is obvious that those who choose to go with their ideas, with their seemingly outrageous schemes, are the winners. So why not choose yourself to operate from the imaginative space? And we suggest that you will be doing so almost totally to reinvent your world.

As will be stated in further discourse, it is not necessary to maintain any sort of belief structure. The freest individual will be one who has the least belief and the most openness to Knowledge. This individual is one who places no judgment on what the mind presents. There is ultimate trust in fantasy, in intuition.

The mind was designed simply to assist in the manifestation of form. The mind is a delicate creature that has a Will of its own if so allowed. We suggest that you as the Self take back the control of mind. It is a simple yet lengthy process.

Spend periods of time where you can simply watch the thoughts that pass through the mind. You will see a varying number of positive and not so positive thoughts go in and move out. Thought patterns move very quickly. We suggest that you ask for assistance in creating only positive thought or thought that will only work for your benefit. Do not judge any of the thought, for thought is only thought, it has not yet been made manifest. This is the place where manifestation can be halted and reviewed.

We suggest that you recreate the thought that is not suitable to desire. For instance, it you want to create love in your life and a thought of hatred passes through the mind, reinvent the thought. Think of an individual or an object that you love and transfer that quality of love to the one that you hate. Then watch the hatred melt away. This simply transfers positive feeling to a darker space. It begins to lighten all of one's thought and eventually all of one's manifestation.

In the exercise previously the imagination was used vividly. As you begin to clean out all of the closets in your psyche and replace them with light, there may be temporary gaps in consciousness. When you are no longer creating painful drama to live through, you will begin to question what is left for you to do. Life may seem empty. This is where imagination is essential. This is where daydreaming must fill the gap.

Know that anything is possible in your world. For eons in time and space you have imposed tremendous limitations upon yourself and others. As you move into light, more and more limitation will dissolve. You will find that you can do anything that your imagination can dream up. If you cannot accomplish a certain task in physical embodiment you will find ways to astrally carry it through. And the astral world will begin to blend with the physical world so much that you may find it impossible to tell them apart.

In knowing that all is possible, the mind can create anything you desire. Let it be free. Do not judge its creations. If there is fear, examine the fear. Use the mind to send light to the fear. Take the fear into your playground and tell it that you appreciate all it has done for you, send it gratitude and love, and send it away. It will have no use in this new life you are creating.

Only those who are connected and completely utilizing the imagination will be able to make the shift into the fourth dimensional realities. Those who choose to remain limited in viewpoint will decay and eventually leave the planetary system, for they continue to play with density. There are many reasons to play with density, many lessons to learn from it. But it is our estimation that you are ready for flight and thus you read this insight only to empower your own wisdom.

We suggest that it is necessary for the mind to be in its imaginative state at least two hours per day in order that it "catch up" from the lost past. Do not impose restriction on sleep either. Sleep is an essential way to practice the daydreams that you create while in waking consciousness.

We suggest that you play with energy, with frequency to create imagination and to enhance it. If you fantasize a scenario in your mind, something that you wish to create, simply take the situation as a whole (take the essence of that situation, not particular facts) and see it in your mind's eye as energy. You may see patterns of light, color, and texture. Make the energy more beautiful by adding light, color, and texture by moving things around, rearranging. This is recreating your experience. This is the process of shifting the energy of a situation enough so that it can fit into your life. You see, you may have some internal resistance to the situation that is still hidden deep within your subconscious Self. There may be resistance or elements in your life that at present will not fit with the new situation. You need not know what these elements are when you work with energy. You simply make the energy of the situation more beautiful and just right to fit into your life. Of course, it may take more than one session; it may take many sessions to shift the energy into the right place.

Do not be surprised if your daydreams and desires have changed somewhat after working with the energy of something. For your guides and Universal forces will shift anything that is not of the highest frequency. If the image that you carry of this certain situation is not of the highest purpose for you, it may be shifted by higher consciousness to maximize your reward. For instance, you may be dreaming about changing your life somehow. The Universe (your personal Universe) may decide for you that you deserve something much better than what you can perceive from your momentary consciousness. The more you play with energy, and eliminate struggle, the more you will have in your life. The more beautiful you become.

It is our pleasure to share with you the secrets of creation, for we will be creating Heaven on Earth together. We need your help in this project. Therefore we suggest to you that it will be necessary to put the pieces in place in your personal life so that we create together only through a state of total joy, of bliss. We want blissful creation. It will be our duty then to assist you in making your lives as ecstatically filled as possible. So Be It.

MENTAL PROCESS AND MANIFESTATION

The Twelve: We shall speak to you today on the topic of mental energies. The mental process which human beings encounter begins "way out there" in twelfth dimension. You see, beyond what we term as twelfth dimension there is no concept of energy. The perception of energy begins at the twelfth dimension.

We want you to know how terrifically brilliant twelfth dimension is. Imagine your planetary sun. If you were to move into its extreme light, this would not be bright enough in comparison to twelfth dimensional consciousness. But from your third dimensional perception, your sunshine is very bright.

As we stated, thought patterns essentially begin in twelfth dimension. But most often you as human beings wish to begin your thought process in the fourth dimension or even the third dimension. Yes, you create often from your emotion. We do not wish to discourage you from doing this, for creation is simply creation, but if you are longing for the highest creation possible, we ask you to step out beyond your third and fourth dimensional realities and create from higher dimension.

The frequency of third dimensional emotion is not as fine as that of higher dimension. Therefore all you need do is take your desire, put it in the area of your third eye. Now you have the idea in your forehead. Leave it there as you go into your meditation, your altered state of consciousness. Hopefully you will move out of any awareness of third dimension. And if you are skilled at meditation, you may move out to the seventh and perhaps the eighth dimension of consciousness where it seems, from your mind's perspective, that there is no form. There is only a sense of being.

With your idea out in the "no form", even more convoluted than usual. It will be created in the highest possible energy pattern, as long as you place no judgment upon what can happen. You may experience that this idea, this thought form that came through originally from your emotional desire in the third dimension, will be blown apart, blasted away in higher dimensions of consciousness. Any conceptual form within an idea will not be able to exist as such in the higher realms of consciousness. But you will then be creating from a most high, high position. It may be that your emotional desire, in the third dimension, has a basic description of what you wanted. But if you are willing to let go of such rigidity and take your idea into higher dimension, you will find that when it comes through your physical dimension it will be much more beautiful than your emotional desire could have created.

There may be indicators from your guidance sources and from your external reality that you are not creating from your highest possible place. We are not advising that you attempt to create from twelfth dimensional consciousness if you are not practiced at that. You are not yet familiar with *seventh and eighth dimensional consciousness*, see page 50. And we suggest that you start by creating from those spaces. It is when you take your idea into the spaces of the seventh and eighth that you must let it go into those spaces, and come back primarily to third dimensional consciousness, knowing that your creation has been created.

Your main challenge at this point in time is to subdue the emotional desire once the idea has been taken to seventh and eighth dimension. It is that the emotional charge, related to any desire can inhibit the manifestation of your creation in physical reality. The emotional desire presents to the Universe a longing that says "I don't have. I am sad. I am angry. I am frustrated. I don't have." And this longing, this creation comes out of third dimensional thought process. "I don't have." Therefore you create "I don't have."

So it will be your biggest challenge to talk to your emotional body. Learn to love it, learn to respect it but do not let it create for you. It is not a creator. And if you find yourself longing or desirous, just remain aware of what is going on. Say to your emotional body, "thank you, I love you. Be with me. Allow me to feel joy, happiness, and even sadness. But please do not desire in the way that you desire. For I have created my idea. I have simply done it from a place of most high. And it will be that you, my emotional body, will be very pleased with this creation. You will see that you will no longer desire. So please, please assist me in dispelling this intense emotional desire."

It is more than likely that your emotion will then say, "Yes I will wait for the highest creation. In the meantime, however, as the emotional body, I would like to generate love and acceptance for all parts of the Self." This will keep the emotional body occupied. And generating love for Self is a very highly rewarding task. It is that you are the most beautiful of creation. It will be necessary for you to know that you are beautiful in order that you will accept and not reject your own creation. If you feel undeserving of what you are creating, you will push it away. It may not come into physical manifestation if you are pushing it away prior to its inception in the physical realm. But it may even make its way into physical manifestation and you could still push it away if you feel undeserving.

So we are asking the emotional body to replace its task of desiring, of longing, (which creates anger and fear) with love. It will then be happy, as it will be doing something very positive for you. And this will prepare you to accept your creation in its totality. This is because we advise you that creation is going to become so magnificent once you can accept it. And the further out into consciousness that you can take your ideas, the more magnificent the creation will become. Of course, that is if you can let go of judgment and your third dimensional perceptions of how this creation must come into being. We do realize that we have given you a hefty task in this discourse, but you always know that you have the assistance of others in your human form, and that of other dimensional energies.

We bring to you the Naguda Force to speak to you on the construction of the *mental gridwork* (imagine a grid, like that which you might see on paper only in 3D form—this grid has planes of light that intersect out in consciousness—imagine the entire air space around you being filled with these planes of light, vertical and horizontal—this is the imaginary version of the mental gridwork).

We are the Naguda Force. We speak to you about wave patterns in consciousness and how thought is created. It will seem to you through a primarily third dimensional perceptive that when you look into thought you look into a seeming gridwork. It may be as if planes of light cross one another and you have a checkerboard. This gridwork is not the thought itself. It is the construct of energy that is the conductor for thought to move through. Thought does not exist by itself. It must be conducted.

As you move through layers of consciousness, the gridwork becomes much lighter and finer. In twelfth dimension, the gridwork becomes so fine that it is invisible to the microscopic eye within your third eye vision. But a thought wave can be created in twelfth dimension and it can be conducted through the gridwork all the way into your third dimensional gridwork. Your third dimensional gridwork is much more solid, much more open, much heavier.

There can be congestion in your gridwork at any dimension in consciousness. There are workers upon your planet who work primarily with gridwork. They are now attempting to unclog the gridwork as far out as fifth dimension. It will not be necessary to do any work with the gridwork beyond that. For this is a very protected holy space. Due to your creation from emotion, from desire, you have caused some congestion all the way up into your fifth dimensional gridwork. It will become commonplace for lightworkers upon your planet to adjust the gridwork for others, for you are the leaders. You are the leaders who correct impairments so that your entire planet will be able to shift its consciousness. When a thought is created, it moves through the gridwork into your third dimensional perception and becomes manifest in density. Therefore, if your gridwork is unclean, is congested, a thought can be misconstrued and therefore miscreated in form. We ask that you, through your ability to spin your consciousness, take this into the gridwork and spin out the congestion. First you will do this within your own energetic field. Then you will notice that when you become adept at spinning you will spin large enough to affect those present within your field. Soon it will not be necessary to be in physical proximity to another in order to spin within their gridwork. And so you will become Masters at this spin and will move it very wide and very large out into consciousness. And you will entirely cleanse the gridwork. Thus your creations will become very pure, very perfect. It is with this that we leave you this session.

See workbook questions for "Imagination, Mental Process and Manifestation."

BLASTING

We have been asked to connect with you and discuss matters of blasting stuck old energy patterns. It is true that when an individual separates its own consciousness from that of Universal consciousness, there tends to be a conjunction of energy patterns within the individual body, which tend to coagulate and bind up in very dense, low-frequency form. What the channel is attempting to take action upon within herself at this time is a process which will quickly and very easily move these coagulated energies through the body, essentially blasting them into fragments and opening channels for higher density frequencies to formulate.

We ask that you sit quietly and put your state of being into a meditative place. Of course, this is becoming very easy for those of you who are practicing enlightenment. Meditation becomes at first like second nature and essentially like the nature of your own being, for you will inevitably practice your life from a meditative state. However if you are not meditating at this time in your life, please begin do so periodically. Please make yourself comfortable within the energies of peace. The energies of love vibrate at such high frequency that the density of the human form is not able to incorporate, sensitize itself to the totality of the love frequency. However, you are becoming much, much lighter in nature. As you clear chaotic energies from the psyche you will become much more open as a physical being. Therefore we ask that you take note of every part of your physical body. Take note of where there are empty spaces within. And choose to fill the empty spaces with the love energy. It may feel as if a tingling is occurring, a great warmth. For in physical sensation, love is felt as warmth, joy. We all know what joy is like. But have you ever thought about entering love frequencies or joyful frequencies into your toes, for example? Your toes need love as well as the rest of you. Imagine that there is a **cylinder** running through your body into the earth, out into the heavens. It is through this cylinder that you allow frequencies to enter into the physical body. And when you request, simply request that a certain frequency be allowed in, it will so happen.

For example, if you request the love energy to come in through the cylinder from both the earth and the heavens, it will be done. But remember that when asking for anything in your life, you must believe that it will be so. For you set up many mental structures that prevent your desires from entering your experiential fields. So take note that if you ask for the love energy to move into your cylinder and fill your every inch with its divine frequency, then first you might have some clearing to do in order to totally accept the love frequency. For if you have hate within your physical or emotional bodies it will have to be discarded before the love energy can bring its way through. This is where we ask that you practice with the blasting techniques, which we are about to discuss with you.

It is not important for you to understand in a mental capacity what is happening when you blast away old patterning. It is not important for you to recognize "oh, this hurt comes from my mother" or "I have been a victim of such and such a crime, and I am still hurting from that incident." It is not important to know specific incidents. It is only important to know that indeed there is hurt, there is pain, hatred within your body. And all it takes is willingness to blast through it. Note also that it may take several sessions to blast away every ounce of darkness within. Let us begin.

Blasting Technique: As you sit quietly within your meditative state, picture your cylinder, which runs into the earth, and out into the heavens. It is through the earth plane and the heavens that energy can be sent to you in massive ways, if you so choose. We are choosing to send the energies of peace and spiritual love through your cylinder. Please take note, as you watch your cylinder fill up with light, if there are any areas of what you might call darkness. Move into that area of darkness. Also notice that there is a small pinpoint of light within this area of darkness. You do not have to know what this area of darkness represents. But please recognize that there is light within that darkness. Move into that point of light within the darkness, within your cylinder. With your will allow the pinpoint of light to grow. You are now within that pinpoint of light and with your will you can enlarge it. You can make it grow very, very large. And once this pinpoint of light becomes so large it will explode. It will BLAST open that area of darkness. Notice the blasting. Isn't it fun? It may be shocking at first, for essentially what you are doing is creating light so that there will be no darkness. If you will, you may move to each and every dark spot within your cylinder, find that pinpoint of light within that dark area, put your will into that pinpoint of light and make it grow larger and larger until it explodes.

Soon you will have no more areas of darkness within your cylinder. It will be all light. Thus any frequency you ask for will come through very easily and joyfully. And once you have your cylinder cleaned out, you will be able to go into your physical being, your emotional body, your mental body, the gridwork and you can blast in any area you choose--eventually moving out into your auric and your light bodies. You may notice that your light body, if you have not been meditating with this principle in mind, may seem very much in a void. It is only necessary to fill it with light frequency. And thus you will know your light body very well. It becomes your best friend.

We wish to bring our statement to a close by asking that you practice techniques of blasting each and every day. For it is necessary upon your earth plane that light workers dedicate themselves to light and not to darkness. We can no longer have darkness and maintain evolution. Please know that when you as an individual take your time and dedicate yourself to your own light work within, you are creating light upon the planet. You are allowing the space for others to move into, which will make it easier for their creation to work with light. That is why we insist upon the fact that you become very, very selfish and do only what creates light for you, for the seeds are being planted all over your planet and within the heavens for a massive, we tell you *massive* transition into light. We honor you in this effort as you honor us. Bless you. We send you light. Keep on blasting!

See workbook questions for "Blasting".

LAYERED THOUGHT STRUCTURE

We shall teach you today a process that is fairly new to your third dimensional consciousness but has been utilized in various planetary systems throughout your Universe. This process is one of creation, of manifestation. This we will label as Layered Thought Structure. We shall teach you how lay in frequencies and build your thought. It is a much more effective manifesting technique to be utilized with the utmost reverence and respect. Let us begin:

First of all you start with a knowingness coming from your heart space. When you just know something is right, you feel it with great intensity, joy and love. It will become impossible to create, (as you enter into your fourth dimension and fifth dimension) without this knowing. You on the earth plane have miscreated much in the past because you often create not from knowing, and rather not from love. You have created just to create. It is a misunderstood concept on your planet at this time.

You shall now begin your creation from this space of knowing, from this place of deep love and desire. Allow desire to wake you up but do not allow desire to create for you. When you know something, you know. You then need not desire. When you begin from the knowing, from your feeling spaces, from your heart, we suggest that you bring this knowing into your mental spaces. For the time being, bypass the communication centers, the throat, the area of expression. You need not express it at this time. Bring this knowing into your mental process, into your intellect. It could be at this time that you analyze some about your existing knowledge. And for a brief time you will take your knowing into your mental spaces and pull it apart so that your physical mind will begin to understand what a knowing is. There will come a time when you will integrate this step into the manifestation process and you'll no longer need to analyze and take it apart to understand it. For you will just KNOW and trust that KNOWING. But until the mind trusts the feeling, of knowing, you will analyze.

There is a sense of excitement when you begin to analyze and understand and see parts of this knowing and begin to trust. There is much excitement in trusting the Self. From this place of mental understanding, you will then express what you want, or what you know, to your multi-dimensional Self and the Universal Forces. It may not be a verbal communication or expression. At first you will understand it only as essence. Of course, your mind likes to picture things. It likes to break them apart and bring details together in your outer world. And this is fine. Know that your manifestation has taken place at all moments but if you create from a place of KNOWING, your manifestation is perfect. Do not forget that. For instance, if you are creating love in your life, the essence of profound and deep love--you will KNOW the essence. And we suggest that if you do not know the essence of your potential manifestation, delve deeper into your heart spaces. Do some work on clearing a path for KNOWING. You have garbled much of the pathway with past hurts and past wounds. Release those so that the pathway is clear. You will begin to know the essence of that profound love you wish to create in your life. And if you are one who likes to analyze, take it into your mind bit by bit. We suggest that the mind likes something to do anyway. And you will begin to see this manifestation in your life. Now, if you have misunderstood love in your past, were pretending to love and did not know the true essence of love, you will now begin to see how you have misloved; how you have created your life from a place of misunderstood concepts of love. We suggest that perhaps you will see relationships that you had created out of need, out of desperation and thought all along you loved. And you loved in your old way of understanding. But that will not be good for you when you begin to see the essence of profound love, you will begin to see the ways that you have created from old belief patterns, from old ideas, from old concepts. This can be fun. It does not need to be a tumultuous process for you. Human beings tend to beat themselves up over past creation. You will begin to see and feel and experience love in a purer sense. Your greatest challenge will be to love purely those creations that you created out of your misunderstanding. This will be a joyous moment for you when you recover the love you have lost. When you can love something that you have previously miscreated, you are truly loving.

You will take this manifestation one step further, because as you begin to see how the essence is beginning to manifest in small ways in your outer life or external vision, you will add just a bit more to your creation. You will begin to see in your mind's eye this essence as energy, as an energy pattern. You will actually see the movement and feel the movement of this essence. It is moving very close when you experience the mind's eye vision of the energy patterns.

And we suggest that you be very creative and very playful with these energy patterns, for you want to make this essence as beautiful as possible. Therefore, we suggest that you lay in frequencies within this essence. It may be that you will have to study frequency before knowing how to do this, but you do know. For you are all knowing and have just forgotten.

Go ahead and lay in the frequencies. Change the energy patterns; make them beautiful. Add color, add scent, and add density. In your mind's eye visualize a frequency that we like to call liquid love. It does have density. It is much like melted gold. You might see it as very flowing, very fluid. You might be able to picture it in your mind's eye and yet not experience any sensation. That is fine. You may continue to watch this energy in your mind's eye. For there will come a time when you will experience it kinesthetically. And then you do know that it is very, very close and within your realm of experience.

So now you are playing with the energy patterns of this essence. And you are changing it a bit, making it better for you, making it higher creation. And you might allow your experience of guides, angels, beings from other realms; you might allow them to help you to make this energy the finest energy. Be careful not to judge your manifestations within this time period, for your physical mind has created a picture of what might occur in this manifestation out of third dimensional consciousness. And when you are creating with frequency, the manifestation will be most pure and may not meet your physical mind's expectations. It may surprise you greatly. You may shift in ways that will bewilder your physical mind. It will be quite amazing. You will begin to do and say things that would make your past personality Self tremble. That is why you must shed your past personality. Your personality will become your soul. So you will no longer be disjointed.

Once you have laid in frequencies and played with your essence as energy and you allow the guides to come in and work with you on this manifestation, allow them to take it with them, for they will take it to spaces that you cannot at this present time and space. And they will perfect it even more and bring it back to you.

They will bring it back to you in layers. It is much like a loaf of bread. For you do not normally eat a whole loaf of bread at once, you eat one slice at a time. Eventually, you have eaten the whole loaf. It will be much like that. They will bring back pieces of your essence and allow you to put them into place. For you do not want it all at once. It would be overwhelming. Eventually you will have the whole loaf. And won't that be fun?

We are gathering as a circuit of manifestation assistants. This is the time in evolution that we have been waiting for. We are glad to see your joy, your excitement. That is all for now.

MOVING ENERGY FORWARD

The start of anything new in your physical dimension requires an energy pattern of motivating force, which must be present in great degree of intensity. It is possible for the human individual to call in this energy pattern. It is energy quite like that of your *Merkabah* (this is an imaginary vehicle or carriage, designed to fit your individual energetic needs for transport through the dimensions of consciousness). It is a driving force— an electrical charge that creates a push. But this push comes up against your energy fields and meets with resistance, which can create a great degree of tension and struggle. It should seem most obvious that when this driving force begins to increase one would allow it to push one forward. That is what *going with the flow* means. As you move into light energies, this driving force will cause all of past creation to melt away. You cannot stay in your past and create your future. If you surrender your physical, emotional, and mental bodies to this flow, to this force, you will find no struggle in letting go, because you hang on to preconceived ideas and beliefs and lifestyles that can no longer suit the life of a light worker. You will forget your life in order to have your life. We talk not of forgiveness, for that is no longer necessary if you have forgotten. Allow the past to dwindle away. Forget it.

Allow yourselves to be lifted from this plane of reality. Go into your future and see it as light, see it as energy, and pull it back into yourself, into your light body, as if it is created in your now. We suggest that you become very familiar with the essence of the energy patterns of each and every experience in your life. For if you go into your future and you find the essence energy of what you envision and you bring it back into your light body, you will have the essence of your future in your light body. And knowing that you are progressing with your light work, your future is bound to be much lighter than your present. And so when you bring your lightest future into your present, your present becomes much lighter. Therefore, you have the future essence in your light body. And that essence will begin to build and attract your future. We also suggest that when you have this essence of your future, that you take it back and run it through your past. When you do this, you make your past as bright as you made your future. And there can be nothing that can inhibit the thought pattern of past experience. For when your past, present and future are all of future essence, you will be living your future. It is also a very quick way to collapse time and space in your perception. When you bring your future into your present, you begin to live it much more quickly. It is important though that you see your future as light filled as possible and not dwell on details. You only need to see your future as energy, and experience its essence in your heart. You will feel it, know it and you bring it into this experience of the present moment. You will begin living it.

This is a very simple exercise. And the more you do this exercise, the brighter your now will become. This is because your belief structures will begin to reorganize to fit your picture, the essence of your future. This all may happen very quickly. So be prepared for a gigantic leap in consciousness when you begin this process. You will be clearing out many thoughts, much doubt, and much fear, for these elements cannot reside within this much light. You will be making your future very, very bright. The mind does not believe that it can be that bright in the present moment. So we trick it. We tell it that we are only playing with energy and we are creating a future, we are not creating the now. But yes, indeed we are creating the now by simply bringing in the energy of the future into ourSelves. And we have our future, here and now. You will begin to correct a lifelong pattern of errors and mistakes. You have previously not been living for your future. You had desires for your future but you did not feel the essence in your heart, in your present. Therefore, it was always your future. When you move the essence energy of your future into the now and you have it in your heart, then your heart will be very joy-filled. We share with you much love and respect as you assist the planet by beginning with your own evolutionary growth. Ascending will allow the planet to live on and become your heaven. So be it.

See workbook questions for "Layered Thought and Moving Energy".

Chapter 8
SOCIETAL CHANGES WITHIN THE DIMENSIONAL SHIFT
By The Naguda Force

We are the Naguda Force. We speak with you today about the changes that will occur primary in this dimensional shift in consciousness. It is important to keep in mind that the entire planet will be making this shift. There will be waves of energy emitted into the gravitational field of your planet that will open up spaces for consciousness (individual and mass) to move into. These spaces will automatically allow for consciousness to rise above the current knowledge of its vibration.

During this period of time, each individual upon the planet will be affected in one way or another. The rate at which an individual is vibrating will determine the space in which such an individual will move into. Understood? Let us explain further.

As this shift in vibration occurs not only on the earth plane but also in Universal consciousness (for all change has an effect on the whole), there will be many upheavals, much "so called" crisis occurrences in your society. Do not be alarmed, for these are expected. It is individual choice however, as to whether or not you will participate in the turmoil itself. You can protect yourself from trauma by working with light and continually raising your vibration through meditation, energy work, visualization and prayer. It is that simple. Just do not allow the mind to wander off course. Yes, you are here to do great works and have an outstanding time, but your main priority at this time is to assist in this ascension process. And for this you will be rewarded greatly.

As the shift is occurring, many individuals are preparing to be pillars of light, which will be placed within your governmental, corporate, and business institutions. It may seem a great task to maintain light within systems that carry so much darkness. But it will be necessary. If it is you, the reader, feeling the call to be part of one of these institutions, begin to honor the call. But most definitely continue to work with light. Penetrate every cell of your being with the frequencies of light so that you will shine this light from within the systems created originally out of fear and resistance.

It will be an exciting time when the larger systems of your society begin to crumble rapidly but will not fall apart. For there will be many light filled beings in place by this time to prevent total collapse of these systems. You know who you are and this call is for you. You are to be honored.

There will also be many who will work from without the larger systems. These are the Light Workers who will be creating new forms, a new world order, which the planet will begin to live by. Do not fear that you will be arrested or torn down for it is time for this ascension, and without your gift of creation the planet could not move into the higher vibrations of multi-dimensional reality.

The Pillars of Light from within and the New Form Creators from without will begin to work together in a partnership never before seen in the history of your planet. It will be a fantastic union of renegades and structurists. You will create a new foundation, which will support all life forms upon the planet in this ascension.

It is understood on the higher planes of reality that once the major part of this shift has taken place in perception we will begin to see one another. We will begin to manifest substantially within each other's reality. We wait for this day because we have much to share with you face-to-face. There are energy techniques that will give you the ability to advance greatly. But it is impossible to give these techniques to you in your limited capacity of language.

Even symbolism within your current awareness is too limited. So we ask that you open yourself up to this possibility. It will be very rewarding for sure.

If you find yourself quieting down, that is good. There is not much to be spoken when you reside in truth and when truth is so simple. It is the mind that complicates.

Let us share with you some of the important factors that will be changing on your planet. As we mentioned before, there will be many changes within government, corporations, and business. They will not deteriorate, for you have fine-flow structures established underneath all of the chaos created by the incompatibility of the people working within these structures.

It will be necessary for systems to work as joint units in manifesting light. It will be up to the pillars implanted within these systems to continue to build the light within themselves and to radiate this out within the systems. The changes will be massive, but will come about with very little resistance once the light workers are in place. It will all be done intuitively with the linear assistance of the rational mind. It can not be emphasized enough that light workers within the system must continue to keep their focus on the light and seek support from light workers both from without and within (there will not be many pillars within so it will be up to those without to support and honor those working in such density.) These systems will change and begin to flow fourth dimensionally. Their products and services will finally support the people. The people on the other hand will insist upon this support so it is a mutual set of circumstances.

Another factor that will change is the composition of your earth plane. It is predicted likely that massive destruction will occur upon the earth. This is not necessarily so. She knows what she needs for her ascension but she is not ready to kick her inhabitants off of her. She needs you as you need her to complete this experiment. Communication techniques will significantly change and alter the way individuals think and work together. If you didn't need to communicate with one another verbally, you would save great steps and much time and space. Creating will become instantaneous, joyful, and much unified.

The channels of sexuality and finance will become very clear upon your earth plane. Sexuality will still serve its purpose of reproduction but it will also be a powerful force in raising the physical vibration. Orgasmic states of consciousness will be easily obtained and maintained within the physical body. Finance will no longer be necessary because in time greed will disappear. Due to intensified psychic development within individuals, those who have remaining greed will eliminate either the greed itself or they will eventually have to take the greed with them through the death and dying process into the next world, a next reincarnation elsewhere. Planet earth, in time, will no longer support the violence.

Children will be born onto the planet with incredible skills of manifestation. These are souls who will contract with light worker parents willing to support the divineness of these beings. For their work is very important.

Physical moves and transportation will become very easy. Each individual will learn the techniques of manifestation and decomposition, bi-location, and astral projection. Technology will be very advanced due to the assistance of other planetary helpers and spirit workers. There are many advanced civilizations throughout your Universe and others that are awaiting your call for assistance. Physical bodies will be very transparent yet radiant. They will lighten greatly. Your plant life will transform to support this shift of physical ascension also. Animal life will begin communicating with humankind, teaching the simplicity of being mindful. It will be a great reunion of the whole on your planet. The blissfulness felt within humankind will propel the ascension even further. It is a good thing, a very good thing.

TIME AND SPACE

We are the Naguda Force. We bring to you explanations about what you call your time/space elements. You will conquer your perceptions of the time/space element. For when you no longer perceive a time/space element, you are able to move through time/space without delay.

Essentially, time is created in the mind. It is present within Universal Mind as well as human mind, but is simply present as part of the whole. It is not an element onto itself. The human mind perceiving itself as a denser field also perceives time as a separate element of creation. This it is not. If time must be of the whole element of Universal energy then it cannot be a hindrance to you on your earth plane. It is only when you think about time that you get yourSelves in trouble and fret. Forget about time. We suggest the grandest experiment on your earth plane will be when individuals no longer wear watches and go simply on that aspect of intuition and knowing. For you have all had the experience of being on time without knowing what time it is.

And yes, you do have your element of sunrise and sunset. This is a significant indicator of time past. We suggest however that if you go with the flow of nature you will forget that there is a time element involved in that flow. And when you forget that there is a time element and simply integrate your concepts of time into the wholeness of All-That-Is you will not experience gaps in your creation.

It is a difficult concept to perceive, to understand when coming from a third dimensional understanding place. And as you raise your vibration and become more multi-dimensional in your perception, you will not perceive yourself as being separate. Your physical body will no longer control the essence of your total being. For it will blend in and assist in your evolution. It will not be a hindrance. It will not be separate. It will be of the consciousness of All-That-Is.

You also create time gaps in your creation by believing old beliefs. If it normally takes two days for your mail to be delivered across country, you believe it is so. But when you forget the old beliefs, perhaps your mail could be across country within an hour. It would eliminate your postal service however, and mass consciousness on your earth plane is holding. It is holding beings in place in a time/space continuum. That is why we suggest that those of you light workers who are serious and determined to raise the consciousness upon your planet (and first of all within your own being) must work with consciousness at levels beyond, beyond your awareness of the Self consciousness.

It may seem a silly concept, one that is not comfortable and also one that you do not understand. But to play with consciousness beyond your own awareness is very beneficial to the mass consciousness. It may seem a challenge to work as an individual and hold spaces open for mass consciousness to move into. But this is what more and more of you crave spiritually. To hold open those spaces of consciousness so that many, many individuals on your planet may shift without doing the intensive cleansing upfront. It is a great task, a very reverent task that you have undertaken. And as you move out of your belief structures that hold you to a time/space continuum, you will be role models for many others to follow. This will be your biggest challenge at this time, to simply trust your intuition, and never to wear your watch. We do not expect that this will happen to you within a matter of days, but when you begin to follow and move to that intuitive voice at all times, you will move into the space of no time, for time is only a perception. Your physical reality is only a perception, and if you want to play with time and play with the perception of a physical reality, then fine. We ask that you do so with much joy and love for your own creation, for that is the gift of physical life. It is your intent by simply reviewing material such as this within your own consciousness. It can be your intent to live with joy, and play with joy, and create with joy.

If it is for your joyfulness that you use time, then you use time wisely. But if it is being used to create misery, gaps in consciousness, feelings of boredom, loneliness and pain, then time is not being used wisely. Time is a hindrance. When you focus on your misery due to the time gaps in your creation, you create a much further time gap. You expand it because you focus on it. It could be a challenge for you to awaken in your morning and follow through your entire day focusing only on beauty and nothing else. If you do this, you will begin to see beauty everywhere you look, even in places where you thought previously were not so beautiful. You will find beauty in All-That-Is and your creation will become more beauty-filled. For what you perceive on the inside, within your heart you create. The mind has the ability to focus its intention, the intent on something other than what might be in your heart. For instance, the mind as stated before can create from emotional longing and desire, a sense of lack. It can create. It has that ability. When you fill yourSelves with light and begin to work with light, it becomes much more difficult to create from lack. You must begin to create from your heart. Then time and space will be in accordance with that creation. You may intentionally slow the process down in your creation in order to understand bits and pieces of that creation. You want to know it in its totality; in its total beauty. For then you are in control of that process of slowing it down. And it makes you the master of your own creation. But when you focus on lack and create from that lack, yes time does slow but you are not consciously intending it to do so. Your longing is to have time speeded up. Therefore it is necessary to remain conscious about all of it. It will be a very conscious creation if you create only from your heart. So be it we leave you now to contemplate upon your heart creation.

See workbook questions for "Societal Changes Time and Space".

Chapter 9
THE TWELVE PRINCIPLES OF MANIFESTATION
The Naguda Force

We are the Naguda Force. We shall now reveal to you twelve underused principles that have been held within the stratum of the *Akashic Records* (the ethereal records of all events that have taken place, past, present, and future) and have long been known and utilized by great Masters upon your earth plane. Access to these laws of nature is now being provided for the important use of elevating the earth plane vibration.

However, we are protecting this information however from any negative mind. Therefore, if the information will not be used wisely, these pages will most inevitably become harder to comprehend. It is only necessary for a few upon your earth plane to understand and integrate the following doctrine. We shall begin.

#1 ALWAYS FOLLOW UNIVERSAL LAW BEFORE HUMAN MADE LAW

Your first and foremost rule to follow is the law that says, "Always Follow Spirit Law Before Following Human Made Law." The frequency component within the Universal Law will always be very high. It will vibrate at a much faster rate of speed than any law created by humans. You will be divinely protected when you follow this principle. Ask that you follow Spirit no matter the circumstance. Yes, Spirit often opposes human law and it will seem a great risk to follow Spirit at times. But it is the only way to create perfection.

When doing the Creation, you will find anxiety and fear and it may seem painful to follow Spirit at times. Know that your emotional and physical bodies have adjusted themselves to the sensations of following human law. Therefore, these bodies will resist when you begin to follow Spirit most holy. Ask your Spirit Self to allow the release of this attachment to fear and anxiety caused by the change of path.

It is inevitable that your earth plane within your next decade will begin to follow Spirit Law most holy. When considering a path and you have two directions or perhaps more, always look at the frequency of each path. The one that resonates most high will be the one to follow. But please note that your bodies will need some adjustment in order to follow the highest path. For you must take all of you along.

#2 LAW OF DETACHMENT

The second principle, which we shall give to you at this time, is the law that states, "do not attach yourself to anything." This is the Law of Detachment. In order to exist in a multi-dimensional reality, you cannot cling to the material possessions on your earth plane. You cannot cling to another person upon your earth plane. You cannot cling to your emotions on your earth plane. And you cannot cling to obsessive thought on your earth plane.

Yes, you are human in nature and you are third dimensional embodied. Therefore, you will have desire, and we say that this is perfectly fine, but understand that desire is often a creation of your lower functions, your emotion, and your physicality. This is why you will want to meet the cravings of these lower functions—but do such by detaching your soul from your desire. This may sound complicated, so we shall explain.

When you come into an embodiment within the physical realm, you do so without your soul present within the body. Little-by-little you have conned your soul into becoming an ego-based personality. When you awaken to this reality, you will find the discomfort of your creation. Therefore, little-by-little your soul must detach from your ego-based personality. When your soul has evolved and detached itself most completely, the personality must finally choose to become soul. This is a great day in your soul's evolution. For it has taken many, many lifetimes and embodiments to completely detach from the personality self and expect personality to become soul instead of soul becoming personality.

This is the law of detachment. In fact, you may find yourself during this process of detaching, very much aloof from what is occurring on your earth plane. It is as if you reside elsewhere in other realms and not within your body. This is a very common phenomenon when you begin your ascension, but it is a necessary process, that of detaching the soul from the personality and allowing personality to become soul. Essentially at this time you will have no personality. You will be only soul, soul acting as your personality.

#3 YOU ARE MANIFESTING ILLUSION NOT REALITY

Creation rule number three. When you manifest, You Are Not Manifesting Your Reality--You Are Manifesting Your Illusion. This is a fun concept, one that lightens the load you carry. For if you KNOW that your manifestations in your third dimension are illusory, you will begin to build an illusion of magnificent quality that will suit your soul's integrity.

Each and every creation in your third dimension is an illusion in that it is separate from source and it only becomes reality when it reunites with source. So keep in mind that this game of earth living is just that, it is a game. Such phantom qualities as pain, dysfunction, discordance, can eventually be released if you know they are illusion, and if you can convince the mind of such. For you have full choice within your manifestation to create what is good. Therefore it is not an evil deed when you wish to manifest anything within your earth plane and it is not reality. So it does not matter what you create. It does not matter to the Universe. However it does matter to you.

Light Workers like yourself wish to manifest good but are sometimes under the misunderstanding that manifesting material things is evil-- it is not--it is fun. Therefore, create with purity and with love, within thySelf. Keep in mind that you are only manifesting illusion and not reality. And you CAN manifest whatever you want. There is also much confusion upon the earth plane at this time, confusion of thought and emotion. This does cause chaotic creation.

#4 LAW OF FOCUS (THOUGHT)

This leads us into our fourth principle, that of the "Quiet and Focused Mind." It is an absolute necessity for the mind to become clear and cleansed in order to create perfect manifestation. Therefore in such times of chaos and confusion and jumbled energies, it is very important for light workers to quiet the mind regularly. In this way you will become very focused in your intent and in your creation process. You will know exactly when and how to create. As the mind becomes quieted and centered you will be able to walk into a room of very chaotic energies and quiet the entire room.

At any given time, do your meditation and watch how chaotic your mind actually is. Watch the thoughts come in and out. Are they focused beautiful thoughts or are they scattered with no thread of commonality? Or are they obsessive, continually creating a manifestation of lack for you? Be very regimented in your meditation schedule. See to it that you meditate daily, if possible three times daily for at least one half of an hour (ten minutes per time) of your time and space. It does take your mind at least ten moments in your time and space to quiet enough, to focus enough, to get at it self.

Once it is contained within itself and understands the workings of Self, you will begin to see direct influence of thought on manifestation. And also, look behind the thought to the intention. For often, your intent is not as high as your soul's integrity must be. But know that if you make seeming errors in your manifestation, note that it is only an illusion, and you can recreate. This is your law of focus.

#5 UNLEASHING THE THIRD DIMENSIONAL LAW OF VICTIMIZATION

Next we shall focus on Unleashing the Third Dimensional Law of Victimization. As you will recall, we talked about always following spirit law before human law. Well, human kind has created a standard of victimization. It has become an average set of circumstances within your third dimensional reality that keeps many individuals trapped in situations where they are unable to meet their souls. Let us begin a lengthy discourse on this process of unleashing.

First of all, it is very important for the intellect to be aware that the individual is victimized in many situations. It is important to see how the victimization takes place. There are many forms of victimization. Of course your first and most obvious form of victimization takes place through physical manipulation of another. Note that the seeming victimizer is not totally free of victimization. For he or she is a victim of emotion, of negative thought.

If one is being victimized physically, it is often necessary to get the emotional support of at least one another person in order to release from the victimization. But in order to free oneself from the victimization of negative thinking, of heavy emotion, one must do it of one's own accord to truly free the mind. It is your mind individualized as you, in third dimension.

There are many books written about pulling out of this type of victimization. And many good provisionary tools available. Many of them are good and essential. You also have support networks within your communities that are good. But in all actuality no one other than you can free you.

Many forms of verbal manipulation take place, victimizing another. The process of guilt and shame and fear are all strategic forms of manipulation. They are very well thought out and put into place by your larger institutions and what you term your media. It is all done with the coercion of the power of money at its top. Many people have had moments of agony and feelings of defeat and victimization by what you call your currency. For currency is just that, it is a frequency. But it has been halted and used manipulatively in order to control another. It's original intent was one of equality, of exchange. "For if I have not time to return your favor I pay you with currency which you can use to treat yourself."

But as the lower frequency energy rose upon the earth plane, money became a tool for coercion, and power, and victimization. This is a very subtle but a very necessary victimization form from which to pull oneSelf free. It is our suggestion that you take a deep, deep look at the ways in which you have been kept victimized by the tool of money.

It will also be necessary on the physical, emotional, mental and psychic levels of reality to cleanse the grief and the sadness, and ultimately the anger related to this victimization. All of this emotion can be transmuted however into that of trust in your higher path, in your Higher Source. The Higher Source is a part of you and it will take care of you.

We do suggest that your currency has a deva (a divine entity that watches over) of its own, a very spiritual light-filled being that you can rely on when you need a favor. We shall call this The

Deva of Abundance. And let us for a brief time allow this deva to speak:

"We are the deva of abundance. Yes. We come to you in an effort to connect with your heart energy, with the energy of love, in that we may work together (love and abundance) to create the most beautiful of manifestations. In essence nothing is eternally created unless it is done with love. And truly your soul does not want creation that is not eternal. It is our energy, the Deva of Abundance that you may contact at any time. You may ask us questions about that which stands in your way. That which we have found to be the hindering source of your creating this abundance is that you have forgotten your Law of Deservedness."

#6 LAW OF DESERVEDNESS

The Deva of Abundance states:

"We shall speak to you now about how much you deserve. This is a very painful remembering for many. For when you realize that yes, you do deserve the greatest of creation; you will grieve over the many lifetimes of forgetting this factor. Do not forget that you are of the God Source and the God Source wants for nothing. For the God Source knows full well of its deservedness.

Yes, you deserve! You deserve great riches. It is though, when you forget love (love for Self and love for others) that you also forget that you deserve. If you do not love yourself and are not kind to yourself, you do not deserve. If you are not kind to another, you do not deserve that other's respect. What gets in the way of loving self is the fact that you have forgotten to forgive yourself for all past wrongdoing. It is a great, great time in this your earth plane for your monetary systems will be changing dramatically. You may even notice an aura, an energy field surrounding your currency, which you have never noticed before. And when you see this aura, know that you are connecting on an energetic level with the currency that you need to create all of your manifestation.

Because of your victimization through the use of money, you have placed a lot of negative emotion, heavy emotion and thought upon your currency, and that must be removed. You will process this and release it and someday will see the energy field. And know that the energy field is of our essence. As you do your meditation daily on abundance, and call us in. For we bring a soft, gentle love energy into your hearts, which will allow you to create with love. We give you much abundance."

#7 LAW OF CONFIDENTIALITY ATTRACTION

We shall now take you into our seventh law, which we will call Confidentiality Attraction. And most simply what this means is that you attract exactly what your confidence puts out. If you are confident that your running shoes will carry you far and fast, so it will be. If you are confident in your work, your work will be magnificent.

Persons in your earth dimension tend to halt themselves in places where they may be overconfident. For instance, let us use the example of the woman who knows her skills as a secretary, she knows these skills very well and is very good. However, she has limited her confidence if she is not moving ahead on her life's destined path. For it may be that her life path has called her to reside in her secretarial position for a time so that she can learn other lessons in life. But it may be now that the Universe is calling out to her to move forward on the Universal path of her destiny. For instance, if she can barely put food on the table for her family, perhaps it will be time for her to move more fully onto her path. Is it a lack of confidence preventing humans from moving into their greatness? Take a look at the environment around you. For as we have stated, you are creating illusion, but if your illusion does not suit you it could be that you are not as elevated in your confidence as you could be. This has been a seeming problem on your planet for ages. For there are some who have confidence beyond what they actually need, and there are many who have very little confidence in themselves.

Take note that lack of confidence is another type of victimization created by the lower energies. For in that lack of confidence there is fear, there is doubt, there is guilt, and there is shame. These are elements created by the lower level frequencies of the personality self.

#8 BECOMING THE SOUL-SELF EMBODIED
Purification of the personality by dissolving it in light

We would like to move into a purification technique using energy, which will rid the personality from this lack of confidence. At the end of this manuscript (Appendix B) you shall find a spiral journey into light. This is a meditation that you can do to help you evolve your personality and bring it up to soul. You will Become the Soul-Self Embodied.

Here we shall explain why it is necessary to dissolve the personality into light. When you begin your awareness journey and the ascension process, your personality will definitely carry resistance. It carries this resistance because it is unaware and afraid of losing itself. For it has seen itself as separate. When you take the personality into pure light, it will dissolve and will no longer exist as a separate personality. It is much like throwing a drop of water into a lake. For the drop is still there but it becomes the lake, it becomes a much larger quantity. This is essentially what you are doing by taking your personality (which is not your physical body, it is not your emotional body, it is not even your mental body; it is a separate entity which has resided in your physical, emotional, and mental bodies; and they have worked together to create your third dimensional illusion) into light. But in order to create from a much higher dimensional reality, personality must dissolve and return to the bodies as light.

You may take your personality into light as often as you need to in order to dissolve everything that hinders your evolvement. It will be a great day when you know your personality as that of light and only light, for then it can rule your physical, emotional, and mental bodies in a very high frequency way. It will not consume, it will only direct. It will not overpower, it will only guide.

Expect dramatic changes in your behavior as you begin your journey into light with your personality. Yes, there may be times when you will go to extremes. The personality is simply acting out old behaviors in the extreme so that you may see them as illusion and release them. So do not allow these behaviors to create shame within yourself, for there is no need to shame yourself. Only see them as cleansing themselves from your personality. For when behaviors (i.e. actions from excessive emotion, violence, out of the ordinary consumption of any substance, etc.) become truly outrageous--if you look at them--you will be given the chance to see how they hinder your growth. What a marvelous time you will have if you keep in your heart and in your mind the realization that you have taken on one of the most tremendously difficult tasks in the evolution of your planet. For you will have no other task as monumental as this ascension.

Therefore, the guidance sources beyond the fifth dimension are very grateful and very willing to assist in your evolutionary process. So get in touch as often as you can with forces beyond your fourth dimensional frequencies. Most of the time, you will find yourself perceiving from a fourth dimensional space of love and harmony, more and more you will feel compassion as you evolve, for that is the wave of energy that is coming into the planet in great waves. The guides are sending it and you are receiving it. You may not perceive it at this time for there may be hindrance yet in your personality self. But as you do your spiral journeys into light, you will cleanse more and more of the darkness from your personality self.

#9 SEEING EVERYTHING AS ENERGY

We have for you four remaining laws or principles all pertaining to the same subject, that of energy. We shall begin with the first of our energy laws; you must always keep in mind that **Everything, Absolutely Everything Is Energy**. And it will be up to you to keep this fact in your conscious awareness. You will begin to see not through the physical eyes but through the eyes of spirit as you ascend. Because the physical eyes are needed in third dimensional consciousness, you will not lose your vision. You will only change the perception of your vision. You will begin to perceive much of the time from a fourth dimensional consciousness. You will see energy flow and energy movement in all situations and in all things.

When you can see (perceive) energy movement, you can predict your so-called future. For you will begin to see flow and patterns in the energy. Mind you, you may not see these patterns in the physical dimension, as there are individuals who can see energy with their physical eyes. This is fine and it reinforces the understanding but it is not necessary. You see energy in your intuitive body and this is how it works. You will shed your perception of third dimensional reality. You will definitely begin to see that third dimensional reality is created from higher dimensional realities and is not possible without those dimensions.

As you move through energy, your mind will be able to clear itself of any third dimensional perception. It is as if your fourth dimension and higher dimensions are gobbling up your third dimensional perception. Yes you will remain existent in your third dimensional physical body for some time, but you will KNOW it as energy. You will treat it as energy. You will treat it as part of the whole and it will no longer be separate in your perception.

So if your physical body is ailing, you will know it to be the result of your multi-dimensional awareness at that time. It is teaching you to open your inner eyes even further. If your emotional body is in an upset, it is teaching you to open your eyes to a wider consciousness.

#10 ENERGY IN MOTION (E-MOTION)

Emotion is energy in motion. And when it flows freely without any blockages, it is an emotion of joy, of freedom, of blissfulness. It is when energy becomes matted or stuck around a thoughtform that is not created from higher dimensions that it becomes an emotion of anger, sadness, or grief. Mind you, it is necessary to clear these emotions and put the energy back in motion. And you will be able to do this when you begin to see everything as energy. And the more you stay conscious, in conscious remembering that energy is always in motion, the more quickly you will move the denser energies through and remain in light energy.

Energy is all that there is. It can move very quickly. It can move very slowly. But it is always in motion. So take a good look at what emotions grab you. If you find yourself often angered, work with energy. Move into your anger. Look at it. What does it look like? What does it feel like? Examine how you can, with the use of energy, change the format of your anger. It is possible, you know. For if your anger looks like a tight little ball, you have the ability to get inside that ball of energy and change its format. And once you change its format it is no longer anger. The faster the vibration of the energy that you put into this ball, the more quickly it will dissolve.

You are also able to do physical healing in this way. Go inside the sore spots within your body and take a look at the energy within that. Go within that energy pattern and change it. Make it beautiful. Put spirals in it if you wish, or lines of light and even explosive balls of light. Just make sure it's light filled. And notice if the sore spot does not change somehow. Within an amount of time and space you may notice that thoughts and perceptions around this sore spot may come up for you. You may be coming from denser negative sources that allow for this sore spot to remain in your body. For the planet is at a very crucial time of clearing congestion. So we must keep in mind that everything, absolutely everything is energy. And working with energy can change everything, with frequency, vibration, light, love, gentleness.

#11 UNIVERSAL SELF-SUFFICIENCY

This leads us to the law of Universal Self-Sufficiency. And simply what this means is that you are God, you are the power of God. You have simply individualized the power of God. And when we say "God", we use this word only as a label. For remember you are filtering information through a third dimensional consciousness at this time. So do not allow your mind to get "hung up" on concepts of what the word "God" means with this discourse. Therefore if you must change God to another label, please do so. For you as the reader do KNOW what your God is like.

God is the Absolute. God is the All. And you are the All. For if everything is comprised of energy, where does energy come from? The God Source. It was a unique invention. A very crafty one. A very creative thought. "Ah! We shall create an entire Universe with energy." What genius. And what genius you are. Do not forget that. For it is all in the divine plan that indeed you will remember who you are and where you have come from. Therefore if you are the God Source (and yes, it may take reminding at times--do not forget to do your prayers, your meditation, your reminding Self that you are of God) then everything within your creation is of God. Everything that you have endured in this lifetime and what may seem to be other lifetimes is of God. You have just forgotten to put light into your creation. And a light-filed creation is much more pleasant than a life created out of ignorance, out of darkness. Therefore you are self-sufficient. You can do it all on your own.

If you are on an island alone, KNOW that you can handle all of it. Of course, it is much more pleasant to be with another, to support one another, and this is good. We do not advocate isolation unless it is chosen. We do advocate however, that when you are without support, you are very self-sufficient because you are of the God source. You are God. You can create anything that you wish to create. And you will begin to KNOW this very well. Your creations are becoming very light-filled upon the planet for those of you doing the light work. Your creations will become instantaneous. For there will come a time when your desire will be so aligned with the moment that you will no longer wish, you will have whatever you need right there with you.

It is very important for you to remember that you have it all within. And if you must use concepts of beings that are without yourself, do so. For it seems to be a time on your planet that many are remembering, but because the information is so very foreign to your physical, emotional, and mental bodies, you are separating yourself from the source of that information. That is fine. But there will soon come a time when you will become the information, the knowledge, the KNOWING. You will "speak truth, and nothing but the truth, so help you God."

#12 THE EXQUISITE LAW OF MASCULINE AND FEMININE BALANCE

This brings us to our last and most beautiful experience of all: The Exquisite Law of Masculine and Feminine Balance. There is no more exquisite blending in the entire Universe than that of male and female. For as you move into the KNOWING of that blending, you may encounter some keen physical resistance, as well as emotional resistance to this blending. This is because on your planet the energies of male and female have been imbalanced. Neither one has been any more powerful than the other. However, the masculine power has been more overt than the female power, which has been subverted. It is an experiment on your planet, and now the experiment is coming to a close. It is a time of great celebration for those of you meeting in couples where one individual carries more masculine energies in the physical and emotional bodies and the other carries more feminine energies. And yet somehow in the union of the couple, you will quickly transcend any imbalances. And although you may live in a feminine body or a masculine body, you will begin to feel very balanced, very androgynous. For you will KNOW the way of the masculine and the way of the feminine. You will put them together. You will no longer utilize only one or the other. It will be a very exquisite blending. You will feel it within your heart. You will KNOW it within your entire being. And you will radiate that to the world. You will find many individuals becoming very attracted to your energies because you will have blended the male and the female, the active and the receptive. You may hear voices, messages within, and you may choose act upon those messages. You will no longer shut out the messages and just go acting about. And you will no longer listen to the messages and not react to them. It is necessary, at this time and space that you listen and you act. It will be a perfect blending. You will feel so whole and you will share that with others. So Be It. We carry love for you.

We have throughout this period of time transcended our own limitations. When our channel began this manuscript, we, the Naguda Force, came through to her with very little emotional component within our energy field. It is through her development over these months, her focus on love and light and compassion that has brought us into connection with those emotions. We have gratitude toward our channel that she has been so dedicated to the light and to service. We made a decision to allow our energies to open up to love and compassion in order to do our world service, for we were feeling much disconnected from the earth plane. The earth plane is a very loving, compassionate energy and we feel it is important to get our work to the world therefore we have chosen to express it through love and compassion so that you will understand. Had it not been for our channel's dedication to this work we would have remained aloof to this fact and our world service would not have been complete. We thank you. God Bless.

See workbook questions for "The Twelve Manifestation Principles".

Chapter 10
ON RELATIONSHIP
By The Pleiadian Brothers

Good Morning! We come to you quite from another world, which is relative to yours but carries a frequency elevated from your human race at this time. That is, in our physical dimension we know that we are not limited to the physical realm of existence and we can carry ourselves out of physical-ness just by intending so. You will get there as humans also. Just be patient and practice your good will service first.

Let us begin this discourse by stating that relationship is simply relative! Funny isn't it that we as physical beings tend to want others to fulfill our lives for us, yet we essentially have that fulfillment within ourselves already. Let us speak about that. Say for instance that as a female you want to meet a man who will bring on good feelings within yourself. No harm in that. We all want to feel good. But did you know that you need no other to produce those feelings? However, when you perceive yourself as separate and not as part of Source then you perceive to need another human to complete the unity. In this part of the human experiment it will be necessary for persons to unite in relationship in order that the healing of the planet can begin. For you as a race still perceive yourselves as separate. Therefore you will not grasp the concept of Oneness until you unify forces with one another.

We ask you to try a mini experiment. Today as you go about your day (or if you can not remember this for an entire day, then for one hour), bring in the love frequency. Bring a felt-sense of love (if you can) into body. Feel it and center it. Then as you go about your day and meet with other people, share that sense with them. How do you do this? We say that it will show in your eyes. The eyes are most revealing. When one is in a loving space, the eyes will appear deep as if you can see right into the soul. When the love frequency is shut down, the eyes will appear glazed over. It will not be necessary to speak to anyone if you do not wish to do so. It will only be necessary to carry (feel) the love frequency. Others will pick it up.

The next step in this experiment, once you can maintain and carry the love frequency easily, is to project it. You can consciously project any frequency you wish. It is a matter of intent. All you must do is consciously intend to project the love frequency and you will envelop others in it. Say to yourself, "I intend to share the love that I feel inside with the others in my life," and it will project to them.

The best experiment then is to follow through with receiving. Oftentimes, humans are good at projecting love but are very resistant to receiving. It seems that because of your illusion of separateness and the unwillingness to open to oneness, that many people put up invisible barriers to prevent receiving love. This often is due to the fact that accepting love has been proven to lead to pain in their past experiences. This keeps one separate, however. If one does not recognize that love creates unification, then one does not accept oneness, of energy as being All-That-Is. You are simply energy with consciousness enough to manipulate and play with it. You can do anything you want with energy. You have done everything with energy to separate. Now it is time to play and watch what happens when you start putting it all back together. Won't this be fun? You are moving as a race into a period of evolution when you will play profound games with the love frequency. You will begin to know the oneness of spirit and walk the oneness of spirit. The games are just beginning and it will be so much fun for you. You will rise above the pettiness of chaos and pain. You will see that love and joy are what you prefer. Do you feel the love frequency as you read this? Then go out and share it with your world. Give it, but most importantly, open to receive it.

Let us give you a scenario: There are many in what professionals who attempt and do give love all day long to their clients or customers. But what happens to the love frequency if the professional does not open to receiving the love that the clients are returning? Certainly there will be people who will not be open to receiving the love that you have to give or they will not willingly return the love. But there are many who willingly accept the love and give it in return. What happens to the professional who all daylong gives but will not receive? Does this professional put up walls with the excuse that those clients who are impoverished in some way do not have enough love to give? It is not so. Those who exist in some way, those whom you might consider impoverished, often have the most love to give. It is the ego based system of "you're not doing it right so I must show you" that gets in the way of the love frequency. Think about how you set up this hierarchy in your everyday lives to prevent receiving love. It uses much energy to keep this illusion alive. We suggest that you lose this one. But of course you have the choice. We send you much love and will receive love from you.

See workbook questions for "Relationship".

Chapter 11
LOVE AND COMPASSION
By The Pleiadian Brothers

ON LOVE

Greetings! We are your Pleiadian Brothers. We are manifest in human form, but fourth dimensionally speaking. You can see us in your mind's eye but cannot yet see us in your manifested physical. However, we do carry a much similar etheric body to yours. It is our calling to work with the energies of love in your fourth dimensional spaces in order that you may move into the most pure, the most beneficial love for that of your planet.

When we speak of love we speak of something that is much grander than what you are accustomed to when you think of love on your planet, for many of you love but do not understand the complexity and yet the simplicity of the energy of love. You see, love is complete and love is very big, but it is also very small. It is a paradox. It contains polarities. It is not opposite however to your definition of hate. It is inclusive. When you feel as if you hate someone or hate something, you actually are very passionate in your hate. If you can examine hate, you may recognize to be anger, jealousy, rage--all very passionate emotion. Hate unexamined can be very destructive, but may be tempered over time with understanding, love and compassion—and certainly the removal of the objects that inspire the hatred in the first place.

In order to get to your most pure love, examine your hate and of course, love it, honor it, and be with it for a while. So we have this foundation of love within love, a foundation of energy that we would like to determine as strength. It is what holds everything up within love. So it is that you cannot have pure love within your heart if you don't have strength. Let us layer on top of that strength a sense of freedom and unity, as one. There must be freedom within the union in order to have the purest love. So if you are free within your heart, within your person, you can have complete and total union with another. And there is no consumption of the one by the other.

We move forward to the element of trust. For it is when you love another purely that you trust yourself. When you trust yourself you trust another. But you cannot trust another until you trust yourself. Therefore if your relationship mirrors dishonesty, some mistrust of another, take a very good look at yourself. Do you trust yourself? It is that simple. There may be many reasons why the distrust is present, but it all comes down to the fact that if you don't trust yourself it will be very hard to trust others.

Our channel has been playing with spontaneity. Being spontaneous at times can be very unpredictable and can create some element of mistrust. For when you do things "off the cuff", and you say things without first meditating on that expression of self, it becomes a risqué sort of life and can feel quite unfamiliar. We suggest playing around with being spontaneous, for it puts the play back into life.

Definitions of love on your planet will soon be changing, will be alternating. We cannot give you at this time a clear estimation on how long it will take your planet to discover and envelop itself in purest love. You are just beginning to get glimpses of what purest love is.

When you speak of unconditional love, you truly do not know what unconditional means. Yes, it means without condition, without limits, without boundaries. But you set up family structures that create boundaries. For you do live in a third-dimensional reality. Therefore, you need walls on your house and you need walls on your family structures in order to maintain your third-dimensional perception. Therefore, we ask that in order to have unconditional love, without bounds, you must have this love in other perceptions of reality. This can be done quite easily.

You can meditate strictly on love. It would be a fun game for you to spend one half an hour per day focusing on what love feels like in your heart. If possible, do not even direct it toward another being. Let it be love, only love. And then begin by applying that love to yourself. This will be the hardest work that you will do at this time. We suggest that you take love into any area of your life where you feel guilty or shamed. For guilt is not necessary. Even the murderer has a choice in the matter. And he makes a choice that another may not make but perhaps he is learning lessons from this choice. Therefore it is not necessary to have guilt over past actions. Guilt only creates a vicious cycle, for when you no longer feel guilty over a past act of behavior, it is probable that the behavior will cease. For then it is not creating the reaction within the Self as it used to. It is as if human nature must do things to get the attention of the Self. It is when you do things out of unawareness that you feel guilty. If you are fully aware that you are making a choice to create a behavior, then there can be no guilt. So you can work with your guilt by shining the light of love into that energy of guilt. For when you exist in a state of pure and total love, you will no longer partake in behaviors that are unloving toward Self and others.

Let us layer on peace to the energy of love. For pure love is very peaceful. There is much serenity in the energy of love. And there is not only trust for the Self, but also trust in the higher flow. For when you are in love, within love you trust the higher flow. You must know yourself very well in order to love yourself purely. When you love yourself you know that you are not alone. Yes it is okay to create community. It is very fine. But often on the journey to finding love you may choose to be alone and transmit love from that space

We share with you this day our love. It is very light energy. It is not heavy at all. That is why you find it difficult to love in density. Therefore we suggest that you spend your time in meditation focusing on love. For when you are in altered state of perception you have no bounds and love can be everywhere and in everything. And you will begin to see love in every aspect of your 3-D perception. And this is the ascension. This is the process you have been waiting for. When you begin to see love in the smallest little detail on your planet, even in war, if you see love then you have it. When you begin to feel love for all that exists in your world then you will ascend. That is all for now.

See workbook questions for "Love".

COMPASSION

Greetings! We are your Pleiadian Brothers. You have asked for us to speak on the topic of compassion and thus so it shall be. Ah! Compassion! Such a wondrous element, one that tests the heart of all humankind. You do not evolve fully until you understand compassion. Let us begin.

Your planet earth has many tests within its energy fields that you must go through. And one of the very last steps in your third dimensional existence is to bring compassion into your energy bodies. You first begin by recognizing within your intellect that there is such a thing as compassion. You see it operating in your world. You see it being expressed by some very high Masters upon your planet. Ah! You say, "I know compassion."

The next step in your evolution is to integrate compassion into your emotional field. Begin to know what compassion feels like. You may have at one time or another felt a compassionate stare from another. Begin to know the essence of compassion and permeate it throughout your energy bodies, utilizing your emotional body to do the pushing.

Compassion is a very deeply intense energy pattern which, when conceived within the emotional body and expressed through the physical, will alter the course of your life forever. Often it is difficult for you of humankind to even conceive of compassion. You have been wounded quite deeply by the density upon your planet. This density causes reaction among the people, reactions that destroy and wound. Therefore, out of your woundedness you say, "I can not feel compassion. Why should I feel compassion? No one has felt it for me." But that is an illusion for you have felt compassion from yourself. Even when you as humankind are in the midst of self-pity you are compassionate about that self-pity.

All it takes is a little transposing. We suggest that rather than sitting in your woundedness and feeling some compassionate self-pity for yourself, transpose this compassion onto another situation, another human being. For if you are in the midst of a situation that causes great self-pity, you tend to perpetuate the situation with the self-pity. It is very necessary for those of you who are doing the light work upon your planet to be able to express compassion for all that exists.

Mind you, we say that you do not need to be in physical contact with anyone or anything in order to feel compassion and in order to express compassion. For the behaviors and verbiage of many human beings does not seem worthy of direct compassion. You must know the bounds upon compassion. What we mean by this is that you can feel compassion and you can express compassion throughout your day in your meditation, but you do not have to give it so whole-heartedly to the one who behaves improperly in your presence.

You see, compassion works on the energetic planes as well as the physical dimension. And often it is hard to love and feel compassion for one who is controlling, manipulating or destroying. And we do not suggest that you must envelop those persons in your physical affection. Oh no! Compassion in this situation will only work on the levels of your soul plane. Remember that within each individual there is a soul body. There are many who have forgotten that they are in actuality a soul body. This is fine. For they have forgotten and will wake up someday.

Therefore we suggest that you express compassion to their soul body, for if you begin to express compassion on the physical plane you will only create tension and disturbance within the ego selves. But if you begin to work with the soul body of another, you will see miraculous changes take place. Now it may be that this person may entirely walk out of your life. So be it. If this person is not ready for the intense amount of light that compassion generates, then they must walk away. There may be someone whose behaviors cause you some distress, and interfering with your light work. Maybe this person is in your vicinity for healing. And all healing begins on the soul plane. Some of the medical (and alternative) treatments used to heal are often only treating the physical symptoms of disease and don't reach the soul. Symptoms on the physical plane are almost always a result of disconnection from the soul planes. But that is quite another topic. As we have said, all healing begins in the soul planes. Therefore as a light worker, it is your duty to begin to work with compassion. Begin to work with compassion on the soul planes by visualizing another soul body. You may see it as energy patterns, light, color, and frequency. You will begin to notice that there may be places of darkness within this person's soul body. This is an empty place where light has not yet been able to enter. And you in your meditation can use your soul to communicate with the soul of another. You can send compassion through the soul planes in this way.

You can tell this other that you very deeply care about them and want their happiness. You want them to move into their own joy, into their own love and begin to create from that sense of self-love. Continue to do this on the soul plane. For it is very exciting to watch the changes in those around you when you have said or done nothing in the physical dimension to make the changes.

Also, prepare yourself for shifts within yourself. For as you communicate with another on the soul planes, you may receive return communication from the other and you may get information about some of your contribution to the dissension between the two of you. Be very careful to listen, be very open and be very compassionate to yourself. For you may find things that have very certainly caused tension in the relationship and have stemmed from your person. It is simply an acknowledgement, and surrounding self in love that these behaviors can change.

Within our planetary system of The Pleiades, we communicate telepathically at all times. And when there is dissension among any of our people, there is a call sent out to many others to work with compassion in healing this conflict. It is very rare however that we do have any discord in our relationships, because we have been through the process, the evolution that you are going through at this time. And we love you dearly, for we know how difficult this transition is for you. We do know this. We have been there. So we are continually sending you layer upon layer of compassion and love.

Continue to work on the soul planes with the soul of another and watch what happens. Make your transmissions as pure and as love-filled as possible. If you are angry, move the anger out of the way while you are doing soul work. Certainly you may ask questions of the other person's soul as to why certain situations have come about. It is definite that you will get an answer. And remember that each and every individual that comes into your vision, onto your path is a mirror for you of something deep within yourself.

It was once said that you must love thy neighbor as you love thyself. So it is very important that you love thyself first and foremost, for if you do not, you cannot love thy neighbor. If you transmit love to another but you do not love yourself, you are sending empty vibrations. You are in all actuality sending vibrations of resentment and hate, not love and compassion. You must first fill your cup with what pleases you and then you can give to another. We are sending you our blessings and our love and compassion.

See workbook questions for "Compassion".

Chapter 12
SOUL MATED RELATIONSHIPS
By The Pleiadian Brothers

Good Day! We believe that many people on earth have become aware for the first time that they are longing for a relationship with a soul mate. A soul-mated relationship varies greatly from what you might call karmic relationships. Each and every relationship that the individual is involved in has its roots embedded in other lifetimes, other realms of existence. You have agreements with individuals prior to coming into this lifetime in that you will share certain aspects of your lives. However, a soul-mated relationship is quite different from the majority of relationships that you currently have in your lives.

Let us explain. Starting in the ninth dimension of consciousness, individual frequencies begin to manifest as groups. Ultimately, when these frequencies are brought through the eighth, the seventh and sixth dimensions of consciousness, they are separated even more. These groups of frequencies in the ninth could be called a group soul, one individual soul grouping. As you travel through the dimensions into your third, you separate the frequencies. But know that there are individuals on the earth plane who once shared with you in consciousness the same soul, the same groupings of frequency.

At this time on your planet, the feminine energies are surfacing after having been repressed for eons. And of course these energies will bring up issues of love, of passion, of receptivity, of nurture. These are very fine qualities. You are all very deserving of these qualities. It is time. In order to save your planet, you must come into the loving self that you are. It is when these qualities start mounting to the surface that you have longing for another to share with you your passion.

You have chosen (prior to coming into third dimension) with another of your soul group to meet in this lifetime and heal the wounds of the separateness of male and female. It could be that male domination and female suppression will lead you to a place of such depths, such agony and suffering, that you will no longer be able to tolerate the intensity of the pain. It could get to this point. Then you will need to begin to heal, to mend. When you finally meet your soul mated person, there will be such excitement and such passion.

You see, in your third dimension, passion is created by unification with your destiny. For you may already know it in your work, you may know it when you look in the children's eyes, you may know it when you hear beautiful music. This is simply because you are reconnecting with your spirit, your soul. Your soul will know when you meet another of your soul group, for the energy created is great passion. For many of you, this type of relationship could prove itself to be very intense, very unfamiliar if you have not yet allowed your passion to unfold. You may run and hide from these relationships for they create an excitement that the physical body is not quite used to. But you will not hide for long. You must come out and face the reality of yourself. For you long to be in your passion. You may be destined to meet one soul mate in this lifetime or several, and for different purposes.

In fact, we shall represent for you a relationship between two individuals who are not soul mated. When you meet another with whom you are soul mated (of the same soul grouping) a passion is present in the relationship at all times. It is a continual wave of passionate frequencies that is present because two compatible frequencies have come together and mated. If a relationship is not soul mated, passion must be created in other ways. This is very misunderstood on your planet. Because you perceive yourselves as third dimensional beings, you feel separate from All-That-Is. And when you connect in a soul mated relationship you have touched upon that unification with the All-That-Is. It opens you to your Spiritual Self. Whereas in a non soul-mated relationship it is one individual of one soul grouping meeting with another individual of another soul group, and there is not necessarily any passion in that. Not to say that these relationships are not necessary or that they are by chance not right. They are perfectly right, for you are destined to meet many individuals of many different soul groups and be with them and share with them. For you help each other out this way.

If you are to be an intimate partner with a person of another soul group, then in order for sexual intimacy to take place, other forms of stimulation will have to be created in the relationship. Since it is a misunderstood concept on your planet, but sometimes you think that in order to have passionate (adrenaline rush) drama you must create struggle for power in the relationship. You create conflict and often very major conflict, for this sometimes seems to generate passion in the emotional field. If you have to stand firm in your own frequency and another is attacking that frequency (simply because this individual is unaware of what he or she is doing), if you must defend your right to be in your frequency, conflict is then stirred and the tension builds. Eventually it builds to a climactic point and then passion is at its peak. You are passionately standing firm in your frequency and so is the other individual. And so you struggle for power in the relationship. Most often one individual will give up their defensiveness (their seeming power) at the climactic point. It peaks and then it falls once again into a passionless state.

If you have ever wondered why some relationships can be so abusive, it might be because the individuals coming together are from very different soul groupings, and one, in search of the lost passion (and unaware of the incompleteness that he or she is feeling) attempts to dominate the other individual. The first individual, also unaware and longing for that suppresses the power within, does not express who he or she truly is, and does not stand his or her ground in the frequency. And the abuse continues until it peaks, until at a soul level, neither individual can tolerate the pain any longer. Therefore it declines. And often in the cycle there is much suffering afterward and there is still longing to be complete.

It is simply an awareness that needs to be created amongst the peoples of your earth plane, an awareness that you are longing to be complete. And yes, you can be complete in your third dimensional reality, but you must open your hearts and your minds to understanding that there are many different ways of completing who you are. You have often gone about it in ways that are destructive.

Having a non soul-mated relationship does not need to be destructive. Only an awareness of the aspect that you are not soul mated (not of the same soul group) will make you aware of the dynamics within the relationship and then healing and love between you can occur.

We wish to get back to the topic of soul mated. Ah! It is such a beautiful, beautiful energy that is created between two individuals who are soul mated and finally come together. Between them they are completing the male and female aspects of All-That-Is. This does not mean that one individual must be male and one must be female. Oh no! It means that they are completing one another. But the majority of soul-mated relationships will be with one male and one female body. For many of you have come to explore the male and female energies in this lifetime.

If you are, say, female, you have both male and female aspects to your being. They can be in perfect balance, but you still have a female body. Therefore, whether your tendency is to bring in more masculine or feminine energies, you are bringing them through a female body. And the female body needs expressing with a compatible body that is also trying to express. Therefore, it is most likely that the male and female bodies in the third dimensional form will come together, but it is not necessarily so. It could be that one person has chosen to be in female body but experiences more masculine energies coming into her body and wants to express them with a compatible female. It may have been chosen as such for this lifetime.

It also may be that soul mated relationships are in no way sexual. Soul mated relationships serve many purposes you see and they may not be life long, and they may not begin until mid-life. It is all in the plan. You have signed contracts through your will prior to moving into the third dimensional reality.

If perhaps you become involved in a sexual soul mated relationship, the power of that relationship, if understood, and used with proper intent, can be quite awesome. The frequency that is being transmitted by this couple of soul-mated beings is healing to the planet. The evolvement of two individuals in such relationship will move quite quickly. It is a fire that will burn off all remaining karma.

As you read this, perhaps you will rush out there in order to find your soul mate. We advise you that there is no need to rush into anything. For it will take place in its own time and place. And you will know.

Our beings from higher dimensions mate with many different of our soul mates. But you, as third dimensional beings, will most likely mate with only one or two of your soul mates at any given time , because these relationships are very intense and you as third dimensional beings do not vibrate as quickly as we do and can not move in and out of experience as quickly as we do. It is true that as you move into these soul mated relationships with the utmost of awareness, you will evolve yourselves into much higher states of consciousness. And in the other realms of consciousness you will find many of your soul group.

It is also true that when you know another of your soul group in this way, and you heal, and with conscious intent, make this relationship as high as possible, you will transmit much love to yourselves, to each other, and to the planet. This is a very good relationship. You will know this relationship, not only by the passion that you feel but also by the ease in which you know one another. If your eyes are open (and we say open, meaning that if you have not blocked who you are through your eyes) you will easily know when you look into your soul-mated partner's eyes. You can also experience your soul mate's frequency by kinesthetic touch —when you touch one another and you vibrate together, there is such union in your vibration that you will no longer need to be separate. You will want to be together.

It is not to say that soul mated relationships go without conflict. No, you have both developed personality characteristics that may get in the way. This may be truly very enjoyable to work out in a soul mated relationship. You can argue with one another and know that you are not going to lose each other. For you are destined to be together. In contrast, in a non soul-mated relationship, you do not return to the same soul, you eventually leave one another until you get into much higher dimensions of consciousness and then you are blended with the All-That-Is.

It is also true that in a soul mated relationship you will join all the forces of your mythological experience. The god and the goddess will be blended. We know of no better way to heal your planet. In fact it is in the destined plan of your planet that soul mates will find one another within these next several years. And those of you who are light workers and know that you are light workers will be mating up very quickly with the soul mates you have chosen to work with. For this is a very powerful bond and the work that you do together as soul mates will bring much expedient growth to the planet. And you will essentially open a space and create models for those who are not yet on the light path. In their longing for the passion, for the soul-mated relationship, for the completeness, they will find their soul mate and begin to grow with light. For those of you who are lightworkers are holding the space for others to move into much more easily than you yourselves could.

When you are soul mated, you will wish that everyone on your planet would be soul mated, for it creates beautiful music because the frequencies will be compatible. As a soul-mated couple, you will enter into relationships with other soul mated couples from other soul groups. You will begin to understand one another and will no longer create the power struggles that a non-complete individual creates in order to find passion.

Yes, you may have one individual from a soul mated couple who is soul mated with another individual, but you as the other part of this couple may not be soul mated with that third individual. It is simply because in your soul group you have chosen to bring in a few fine frequencies and when you soul mate with another from your soul group, this person also carries those frequencies. But you all carry more than just those frequencies. So you may find yourself very compatible or soul mated with a second individual with whom your first soul mate does not completely resonate, but will feel and honor that connection between you and your second soul mate.

We encourage you, at this time, to open to the true expression of yourself. By this we mean, get very much in touch with your frequencies. Often emotional trauma or pain can muddle these frequencies. We suggest that you do emotional clearing so that your frequencies can vibrate at their finest, finest essence. You will be attracted to your soul mate when you are vibrating at such fine essence.. You will come into physical proximity of one another. And you will know. There is no question.

We leave you now with profound thanks for hearing us. We wish you much love and passion in these days to come in your soul-mated relationships. So Be It.

See workbook questions for "Soul Mated Relationship".

SUMMARY
By The Twelve

And now it is time to close this work with an explanation of how you may use the guidance from realms of existence other than your third. You must be clear in your intent. And also you must have worked with light enough that you have cleared your mental and emotional fields, and thus your physical.

You must anticipate the altered state of consciousness to be with you at all times. For it will seem as if you are walking in a dream state. And yes, it is true that the waking consciousness and the sleep time consciousness will become blended. You will misrepresent yourselves as being in waking consciousness when in all actuality you are in your dream state. You all know how creative the dream state is. For nothing is impossible in your dream state.

This is what will be happening when you are awake. This will become a great experiment in manifestation. You will open many channels between yourselves and the realms beyond the third. Know that we are with you at all times. Never forget that. For we are part of your consciousness, and all you need do is be receptive to your own consciousness. But if there are parts of your consciousness that you are afraid of and then you will not be able to access other parts as well, parts that could be very enlightening and very wonderful. So essentially we say that you must eliminate fear and do not judge yourselves. For this is the hardest experience, the harshest of experiences. When you judge your experience, you create shame and you feel guilty. Then you must hide from yourself.

We cannot have shame or guilt if we want to transcend and move into higher realms of consciousness. You will operate primarily from a fifth dimensional state of consciousness when you allow all parts of Self to blend, when you allow yourself to be who you are. It may be that you have persons in your life who judge you when you are being truly expressive. Remember that these persons are only showing you the parts of yourself they are judging. Do not judge yourself, for you have come to experience all parts of experience. There is nothing not to like in experience. Sure, once you realize that certain behaviors and attitudes are destructive, you will want to change them. But do not judge them for they are not destructive in themselves, they are only destructive when you place shame and guilt upon yourself for having acted out these behaviors.

We suggest that you honor them and respect yourself for opening up to accept these behaviors. It is a great being who honors all parts of Self. Forgive yourSelves. That is the most important aspect in third dimensional consciousness that needs to come to light. You often go about forgiving others but you forget to forgive yourself. You are the most important in this your time and space. If you do not forgive the most important, you stay angry and hide in fear.

There is light that you can access, a light frequency that will assist in this forgiveness process. Call upon it, ask for it and you shall experience it. It is a movement of light waves, which move much like ocean waves, like the tide it moves in and back out. It washes clean all of the wounds within your heart. It is a very gentle light and contains many brilliant colors. Let it wash away what you perceive as sin. There would be no sin if you would not judge. There would only be experience.

We advise you once again that no experience is destructive in and of itself. It is the emotion that you create about the experience. The judgment that you place upon yourSelves is very harsh and keeps you from seeing the light. For when you are creating an experience you do not like, you can transcend that experience into one that you like, that you do prefer. You will create the same intensity but with a much more practical means for growth.

There is much light work to be done upon your planet. And we congratulate you for being among those who are at the forefront of creating this planetary shift. There are many of you upon the planet at this time. We suggest that you meet on the gridwork at various times to keep your heads above water, so to speak. In this way you will not get lost in the sea of emotion and mental manipulation that is about to come. For many are still unaware and do not realize the intensity of your light. Of course they feel it, they sense it and may attempt to keep you in darkness. But this cannot be done, for you are of light. If you truly work with light and manifest with light, there can be no darkness. And yet you may still have periods of time when it seems that you are still creating from darkness. It is fine. Do not judge that. Become aware, forgive, and go on, and recreate with light.

We appreciate that you have chosen to listen to our message. And we know each and every one of you out there. We are available for service to you. All you need do is ask. So Be It and enjoy your creation.

Appendix A
TRANSCENDENCE JOURNEY

Yes. We have combined our energies as the Twelve, Talemahe'ke, the Naguda Force, and The Pleiadian Brothers, along with many other spiritual beings and guidance forces to bring to you the Transcendence Journey.

We caution you. Do not do this journey until you have completed the material in this book. If you are not at a consciousness place that allows for complete and open acceptance of this material, you will not be able to achieve transcendence. In fact, you will not even understand the complexity of this discourse, of this journey. So it is best that you comprehend and begin to experience and live the material in this book before attempting this journey. We shall begin.

Hold in your hands an object of power. Whatever it may be, a crystal, an amulet, or perhaps even a stuffed animal—whatever feels powerful to you. Hold a physical material object in your hands. Close your eyes and quiet your mind. Begin to feel your body, your physical body, dissolving into nothingness. Do not however dissolve the object in your hands. In fact you may leave your hands upon this object and dissolve the rest of your body. Become one with the energies around you. Simply dissolve. Allow the energies of multi-dimensional reality to absorb your essence. Become all of reality.

Once you have dissolved your body and become one with the energies around you, you will find it very easy to go into consciousness beyond that of the third dimension. We suggest that you attempt to blend with that of your ninth dimensional consciousness which will feel like nothing. You might feel as if you are in a void space or an abyss. Yet, you might feel the sensation of big energy here. What do you feel?

In your ninth dimension your energies will feel very free, very floating, very non-existent. If you move one layer out into the tenth dimension, you become one with everything that is. Let us ask you to bring your energies back now a little bit closer to your physical dimension, perhaps to your fourth or fifth level of consciousness, where you still experience a separate identity. And when you make it back to fourth or fifth bring, into your consciousness a situation in your life that puzzles you. If there is another person, another being involved in this situation, bring that person into consciousness.

Now take this situation or person and move back out into your ninth dimension. Both bodies or the situation and your body are dissolving. They are becoming one with the energies. (*Pause*)

Now take them out into the tenth dimension where there is no individuation left. There is no situation. You are free. If you like, you may move it into eleventh and twelfth dimension where the energy is so absolute, so All-That-Is that nothing of you will exist, but all of you exists. You have completely merged with this other being or this situation as one. It does exist, and it does not exist.

To go beyond the twelfth, you will experience such expansiveness and may not remember the existence of third dimensional consciousness. So we suggest for the time being that you play only out into your twelfth and do not go beyond until you are skilled at accepting these realities.

You may stay in any area of consciousness you would like, but we shall bring you back at this time layer by layer. Step back into your eleventh layer of consciousness. You may experience just a bit more constriction of the energies than in the twelfth. It is expanse but it is still contained. In the eleventh, you may begin to experience light as a visual or sensual energy, but there is not much to ascertain yet in the 11th dimension. It is quite formless.

Then you step into your tenth. This is where you begin to experience frequencies of joy and ecstasy. For joy and ecstasy are frequencies created in the tenth dimension in order that you, once you move into the third dimension, can accept the constraints of denser consciousness. In tenth dimension, you can pull in frequencies of joy and ecstasy. This is where they begin. For beyond that there is no need for joy or ecstasy.

Bringing you down into the ninth dimension of consciousness. We begin to experience subtle hints of a separate identity, yet it is so vague, there is not clear-cut detail to be pronounced. Remember in the ninth dimension you might feel a void or extreme energy sensations. Each individual encounter in the ninth may bring different experiences with it.

Let us bring you into your eighth dimension of consciousness. This level of consciousness is very symmetrical. What is on one end of frequency is also on the other end of frequency. Much like your figure eight. Very symmetrical, very even. It is at this layer of consciousness that you will find justice, equality. It is in the eighth dimension that you can begin to work on situations or relationships that are in your everyday, third-dimensional life. Visualize a situation that you struggle with or a person with whom you might have a conflict at this time. Play with the frequencies of this symmetrical flow. You and your situation, or you and the other person, will move very equally through this layer of consciousness. Know that you are bringing this energy of the eighthinto the consciousness of yourself, the situation and the other person. It feels very smooth, very wonderful. This is the layer of justice, of equality.

Now let us bring you into the seventh layer of consciousness, where the gridwork begins to set up. For it is in your mind's eye that you will experience the upper level of the seventh dimension as being very free flowing and very non-structured. But in the lower layer of the seventh dimension, you will begin to see a gridwork. This is where the opening for bringing in your experiences from the outer layers and begin to trickle them down into third dimension, into the thought, into the mind of your consciousness.

Bring them through the gridwork into the sixth dimension of consciousness. In the sixth the gridwork sets up even finer, even more solid. You need not spend much time in the sixth. The sixth dimension of consciousness holds a space for correcting mind, correcting your belief systems. If you have some belief structures that are preventing or blocking, or causing conflict in your life, you play in the sixth dimension of consciousness because it is a very pure form of gridwork. You may stay there as long as you like in order to find pockets of energy that will help you to smooth out your attitudes that are creating conflict in your third dimension.

Let us move to the fifth dimension of consciousness. As Talemahe'ke has told us previously, this is the layer where the graces begin to set up. If you live without an essence of grace in your third dimension, you cannot move into your transcendence. So fill this situation, or the other individual, and yourself with graces while you are in fifth dimension. And you do know how to do this from prior discourse. There you will fill with grace.

Then we will take you to the fourth dimension. This is where physical reality begins to set up. For you can see the duality in fourth dimension. You can see how things can be pulled apart and examined, but they can also blend. It is a choice, a free will choice whether you have the blending take place or not. You have a situation with you, or another being with you at this time. And our hope is that you wish to blend the energies, rather than separate the energies. And that is why you brought this situation or person with you out into multi-dimensional consciousness.

So begin in the fourth dimension to blend your energies. Blend it and meld it. Remember you are not completely physical at this point, so you blend very easily. You are very gentle with one another. Yet you may pull apart to examine one another or to examine the situation. Good! You have done a good job. You may stay here as long as you like. If it feels good to blend, stay. Stay until you feel completed with the blending process. Stay!

You will also experience from this blending a profound sense of love and compassion, for yourself, the other individual, and the situation. For blending creates love.

Now we bring you back to your third dimension, physical reality. Remember to bring your body back for you will need it in these days ahead. Practice this journey over and over again. It will bring you a very quick enlightened and easy way to transcend situations that cause conflict in your outer world. So Be It. We wish you much love and accomplishment with this your ascension process.

See journal pages in workbook for "TRANSCENDENCE JOURNEY".

Appendix B
THE SPIRAL JOURNEY

Good day! We shall now take you on a journey of the spiral. It is important to keep in mind the intensity with which you are about to do your living experience. The spiral journey will assist you in evolving your consciousness to a place that is more accepting of such intensity. We shall begin.

As you sit in your meditation, begin to focus your energy in your heart space. Draw your attention to the center of your chest and begin to push out, to clear, to make more beautiful, your heart energy. From the point of the heart, begin to transmit energy all around you in a circle. You may want to use color, vibration, frequency and light to transmit from your heart center. As you get this circle in motion, it begins to create a spiral all around you, for you are cocooning—spinning a cocoon all around your body. Imagine the spiral going upward into the heavens and down into the earth. You reach all directions, but for now we take you up into the heavens and down into the earth.

This spiral is beautiful. Remember to fill, from your heart space, the entire spiral with beauty and love. As you spiral upward you begin to see the spirit realm with clarity. You begin to spiral into God, into All-That-Is. You begin to spiral yourself into that void space where there is nothing, yet there is everything.

Examine this space. Begin to notice what it is like to be nothing, yet to be everything. If you were in a waking state of consciousness at this time, the energy here would feel quite barren. But since you are in your meditative place, you can take in the entire experience of this voided space and feel good with it. Be there for a time.

Know that at any time you can leave any space and you can follow your spiral either upward or downward. Let us take you downward into your earth planet. Spiral down, down, down. What does she feel like beneath her surface? She has heat, she has cold, she has light, she has vibration, she has living entities throughout all of her being. Take some time and watch your Mother produce her beauty. If you will, your Mother planet is the void. She is the same as the heaven we just touched. All of energy is just that, it is energy.

Now we bring you back up the spiral and back to your waking state of consciousness where you can perform miracles in your daily lives. And remember that at any time you can take the spiral upward and downward. And if you wish to practice with spiraling outward in any direction, please do so. Remember to keep the spiral in place and always spiral from your heart space. So Be It.

See journal page in workbook for, "Spiral Journey".

DIMENSIONS TABLE
These definitions of the dimensions are given to us as a reference for use in this book as they relate to the Dimensional Ascension material presented.

Zero dimension ....All and Nothing

The cosmic glue that holds it all together stems from zero. It might be proclaimed as the Alpha/Omega, God, the Highest Power, but it is the invisible force that allows for physical and non-physical existence in our Universe

1st dimension...Darkness, defined by light

Thus begins creation in the first dimension. Without light there would be no darkness for comparison. This is the initial phase of polarity not clearly defined yet because there is no depth to the perception, but nonetheless a presence of duality is felt here.

2nd dimension...Energy

The energetic dimension. This is where energy draws unto itself more energy culminating in the beginning stages of matter. It is compared to a magnet that uses a baser level thoughtform to pull matter to itself to begin form. The beginning of attraction is here.

3rd dimension ....Perception, Time and Space

This dimension allows for conscious perception of form. In order for this perception to exist, consciousness must contain itself in an active physical form of some sort, which has an electrical reception/interpretive device (i.e. the brain) in order to clarify and define perceptual information. This is where time and space can be perceived.

4th dimension ....Frequency

Once perception has firmly solidified conscious matter within its interpretation (in third dimension the mind can perceive form and interpret what that form might be), then it is taken apart and analyzed in this 4th dimension. This is the dimension which clearly defines the shadows and allows for depth perception. This is the dimension of the psyche. Psychic perception is gained here and frequencies can be examined and utilized for analytical understanding and placement.

5th dimension ....Light (in various forms)

From the 5th dimension come various forms or gradients of light, allowed through to the third dimensional level so that consciousness can define itself correctly. One particular form of light may increase understanding of a perception of a certain process, whereas another type of light may inhibit or hide that understanding.

6th dimension ....Higher Will

It is here that personal will dissolves completely. There is no more form or personal choice. Tapping into the 6th dimension allows for complete absorption into the power that we might call God or the Higher Power. It is not the "highest" power in this our Universe but it is certainly beyond the intelligence of the human power.

7th dimension ....Absence of Form

When reaching the 7th dimensional consciousness, there is no concept of form. The physical body disappears and there is no more "life" as we know it in human perception. This is the best place to dissolve major issues and/or blockages that inhibit growth. But to be careful, as once the personal consciousness taps into the 7th the understanding of what/who it was before will no longer be relevant. Without grounded consciousness in the physical dimension, play in the 7th could render a person confused and dazed. It should be noted then that only an experienced light worker should delve seriously into the 7th dimension and beyond.

8th dimension ....Spreading the Mustard

Human language is inadequate to define matters beyond the 8th dimension. Spreading the mustard is the only feasible explanation of the 8th, because it is just like making a sandwich here. Without the spice and good flavoring of the mustard, the sandwich is bland and has no charisma. The 8th dimension is the spread that enhances all of creation. Use this energy to spruce up a mundane, tedious experience.

9th dimension ....The Filter, the Allower

The 9th dimension is the layer of consciousness that allows intelligence from All-That-Is to filter though into the more understated perceptions of dimension. Without clear passage through the ninth layer, human understanding of how the Universe works is much distorted and becomes twisted when played out. It is suggested that the experienced light worker do clarifying work in this dimension.

10th dimension ....Mind, Higher Thoughtform

Although there is no form in the higher dimensions, there is still thought. In the 10th dimension we begin to see how thought is created and developed for use in manifestation of particular matters. It is the most prime example of how intelligence works correctly. A very high level of analysis can come from examining the 10th.

11th dimension ....Completion

The 11th dimension begins the completion of experience from human comprehension. It is here that we can fully dissolve into what our perception of nothingness might be.

12th dimension ....Buried in Form

The 12th dimension yet gets lost in human interpretation. In time the DNA channels will be open such that we will even understand this dimension and be able to use it to interpret and correct our manifestations in the third dimension. At this point in time we can tap into the 12th as the gateway to future and farther dimensions and use (without exact understanding or interpretation of) for healing and perfection. The 12th is available in all form and can be felt (via emotion and intuition) but not yet seen.

A

C

D

G

I

L

M

N

P

S

T

V

DIMENSIONAL ASCENSION: THE COMPANION WORKBOOK

A cooperative work by The Pleiadians and Companions and Jules Kennedy

This workbook corresponds to the material in <u>Dimensional Ascension: Multi-Dimensional Living for Light Workers</u> and is dedicated to all the committed students of this Ascension Earth Walk. Bless you and may God's Light shine brightly upon you in these challenging but de-*Light*ful times.

DIMENSIONAL ASCENSION COMPANION WORKBOOK
Table of Contents

INTRODUCTION TO THE DIMENSIONAL ASCENSION WORKBOOK

Welcome to <u>Dimensional Ascension: The Workbook</u>. This workbook is a companion, a helpmate for the book <u>Dimensional Ascension: Multi-Dimensional Living for Light Workers</u>. The workbook questions are referenced after each appropriate section within the book. You will discover throughout these pages that you will be stopped to answer questions about the material you have just read. It will be important to have a notebook or journal handy to expand on your answers to these questions. When we are working a spiritual path, our visions and direction can become cloudy. This is often due to expanding consciousness. A state of confusion signifies that internal shifting in perception is happening. This is good, but oftentimes can be stressful without tools for understanding. This is why the *Dimensional Ascension* material is being presented in this manner.

HOW TO USE THE WORKBOOK

This process works best if you read <u>Dimensional Ascension: Multi-Dimensional Living for Light Workers</u> in its entirety first, grasping as much of its message as possible. It is recommended to skip the workbook pages in the first reading of the book. The second round of study with *Dimensional Ascension* then involves the workbook, to be used in group process or individual study. There are three segments in the workbook, including ten work sections for the first two segments and six sections for the third segment. In each section, the student will answer approximately five questions. Each section corresponds to particular pages in the *Dimension Ascension* original text, followed by a workbook question page. A brief synopsis of the intent of the particular section questions are listed at the beginning of each section. Begin by reviewing the specified pages in the *Dimensional Ascension* text and follow up by answering the specifically directed questions in detail. The workbook can be used to help integrate the Dimensional Ascension material, and can be used by the individual in any creative way desired.

INSTRUCTION FOR FACILITATORS OF GROUP PROCESS

To use in group format:

1. This format works best if there is a qualified facilitator for each group session. Qualification means simply that the leader of the group has indeed studied the *Dimensional Ascension* material in before holding the class. Some of these questions can be quite personal and leave individuals somewhat vulnerable. Therefore it is essential to have a facilitator handling the group sessions who is comfortable with group dynamics, has a great deal of detached compassion, and knows how to sensitively handle emotionally charged issues within a group setting. The facilitator would ideally be experienced with and have an understanding of multi-dimensional realms of consciousness. This would generate an intuitive flow for the group, which allows for greater integration of workbook material.

2. The group could begin with segment one, section one. Read the material out loud or silently, answer the questions individually (making sure there is enough time allotted for reflective thought and written response for each question), reforming as a group to discuss the questions together. Perhaps several sections could be worked on during each group gathering.

   An alternative to the previous group format would be to read individually, prior to the group gathering time, the material in <u>Dimensional Ascension: Multi-Dimensional Living for Light Workers [use italics, not underline for a title],</u> answering questions to previously set sections, and then discussing findings as a group. This allows for more individual privacy and unlimited time to work with the questions. However, it may cut down on group cohesiveness, depending upon the energy make-up of each group. These format styles for the group can be discussed as the work with *Dimensional Ascension* goes along. Coming to the group prepared allocates more time for individual process, which is good for introverted people, but not as effective for the extraverted student who may learn more in group interaction rather than alone. A good test for this may be to try each method once and see how the group interacts.

3. It is a good idea for the group to begin each gathering with a brief prayer or special meditation and to end with a closing circle of prayer or meditation. This builds sacredness, serenity, and cohesiveness into the group which are necessary components for inner work at this level.

4. Facilitators should be aware that the material will trigger different responses for each individual. Some students may go only so far with it and drop out, only to pick it up some years later. Others may become bored with the material and work beyond the group pace. Each individual learning style and integration rate may be different. Although for this type of work to succeed on a global scale would demand cooperation and respect for differences amongst people, it is a good experience to work cooperatively in group format to integrate and reciprocate the lessons learned from the ascension process. No two people are alike yet we all must learn to live in unison with one another.

   Further material and accompanying guides on Ascension is forthcoming from the author. There will be future books, meditation tapes, an Ascension deck of reading cards and more, to be used as supplements to this material. Enjoy the *Dimensional Ascension* process.

Segment One:
GRACE
Section 1: Introduction to Ascension

The purpose of this section is to clarify the individual Light Worker's understanding of his or her personal ascension process as it relates to the *Dimensional Ascension* material. Also an understanding and openness to channeling will be necessary for the student to work with this particular material.

#1. What is your personal understanding of ascension at this time?
What do you hope to accomplish by utilizing these particular ascension tools in your growth process?

#2. After reading the introduction to *Dimensional Ascension*, what are your impressions or feelings about channeling as explained? Please be clear about your reactions to channeling in general. It will be important for you to be honest with yourself about any reservations, irritations, anxiety and/or excitement you sense before working further with the material. Knowing this will set the stage for your learning.

#3. Do you channel? If so, explain and define your experience. If you feel that you do not channel, would you like to? And how to do plan to open your channel?

#4. What do you think you need to change within yourself (i.e. attitudes, beliefs, behavior patterns) or what baggage (physical, emotional, and mental) do you need to rid your life of in order for it to be lighter? What relationships do you need to heal, clear, discard, or attract in order to make room for your light work?

#5. Are you prepared to work with light (ascension technique) to improve your life? Are you ready to accept the changes that a multi-dimensional reality will create in your life?

GRACE
Section 2: Understanding Purpose

This section will assist students in becoming comfortable with the easiness of grace. When one is aligned with their designated soul purpose, life becomes simple, easy, joyful, and complete.

#1. Do you understand the power within? Do you feel yourself connecting with grace as you work with this book and/or other sources & forms of the light work?

#2. Do you believe that all that you do should be done with ease? Is ease too difficult for you? Explain.

#3. What do you believe is your "soul" purpose in this lifetime? Contemplate upon your God given gifts.

#4. What is your understanding of Divine Creation? Do you experience grace in your day to day activity? Give examples.

#5. What is/will be your contribution to the Divine Plan?

GRACE
Section 3: The Feminine

Utilization of feminine energies will be very important in this time to come on earth. We will need to listen with our hearts, minds and intuition and act on the messages received. The purpose of this section then is to open the student up to the feminine side.

#1. Do you spend much time receiving? On the material plane is it easy for you to accept gifts from others? In regard to spiritual matters, how easy is it for you to accept God's gifts?

#2. Does any part of your being need attention right now? What is it requesting and how can you attend to those requests?

#3. How open is the circle of light (refer to page 15 of Dimensional Ascension) above your crown charka?

Sit in meditation silently and in your mind's eye visualize this circle.
Energize the circle with light and open it fully, much like a ring of light shining upward toward the sky, outward as far as you can and downward into your body. This will allow your Soul to speak to you freely.

#4. Is your solar plexus (the area right around your navel-the third charka area) free from discomfort and disease enough to house your soul?

On a daily basis (until it becomes clear) visualize this solar plexus area filling with light. Also generate a frequency of love and fill this area with love. Pay close attention to the experiences (situations, relationships, communications, etc.) in your life as you begin to welcome your soul into your physical body. You are beginning to express your being as soul at this point. It will be important to keep the solar plexus clear and unobstructed.

#5. Do you love yourSelf? Do you respect yourSelf? Do you know yourSelf?

Section 4: Understanding Energy of Grace

This section will prepare the student for Grace. It leads the individual into mental spaces, which are conducive to the energy of grace. It helps to set up mental receptivity.

#1. What does grace feel like to you? What is your understanding of grace and how does it (or has it) operated in your life?

#2. As you meditate on peace, what do you experience?

#3. Do you have guide sources which help you to walk in a state of grace?

If you have not yet gotten in touch with your guides, angels, or whatever works for you, practice daily to quiet your mind and imagine your heart being filled with love and peace. A sense of serenity should fill your being at this time. It may leave your awareness when you once gain busy your life, but you can get back in touch with it by simply recalling (bring to your mind and senses) your experience in meditation.

#4. Do you experience resistance to grace? Examine this resistance. What is it and how might this resistance be related to your past experience?

#5. Imagine at this time your future Self. Who will you be? How will life be for you at this future time?

If there is unpleasantness in your future experience, remove it by adding grace to your energy field in meditation. Bring this future Self experience into your present (now) experience and see how it feels.

GRACE
Section 5: Integrating Grace

Once grace is understood on a conscious, mental plane, then it must be integrated into the emotional and physical bodies of Self. This section helps the student to integrate grace by answering the following questions, thus opening up the mind via the triggered responses. Contemplate these seemingly simple questions thoroughly.

#1. What does integrating grace mean to you?

#2. What does intensity of grace mean to you?

#3. Do you have resistance to the intensity of grace? Explain.

#4. Do you have resistance to (an obsession with or fear of) density? This in itself can create the illusion of more density through trauma or negativity of experience, heavy emotion, or anything that ties your focus to it and away from accepting grace.

Answer this question as objectively (as if you were your own therapist) as possible at first, followed by an inner more subjective look. This will ease the resistance to the emotional impact of the question.

#5. In meditation, imagine a brilliant light being discharged into your aura, that energy body several inches out from your body. Visualize this energy field being filled with light. What does this bring up for you?

To experience bliss is to open to the gracious energies. This section delves into bliss and back out again.

#1. Can you experience bliss? Do you experience bliss? How do you move into bliss?

#2. What happens to you after a blissful experience?

#3. Do you ever crave bliss? What do you do to attract the blissful energies into your experience? Contemplate what works for you and what does not when attracting blissful experience?

#4. When you meet another person, do you ever contemplate that this person may also be who you are?

> *Your consciousness is bringing all of you to you in the form of external events in order that you may integrate all of yourself.*

#5. Do you now understand energies of grace? Do you feel as if you have integrated grace?

GRACE:
Section #7: Becoming Grace

The intention of this section is to make it easier for the light worker to wear the energies of grace, meaning that to wear grace is to become it.

#1. How much capacity do you feel you have for love?

#2. Do you understand what Talemahe'ke means when she talks about wearing her energy, the energy of grace? What is it like for you to wear grace?

#3. Do you know any starseed children (children of light born with great capacity to love, that never forget who/what they are no matter the environment around them)? What can you or have you learned from these children?

#4. Are you able to align your personal will with the Higher Will? Are there any issues that you are unable to bring into alignment? Explain.

#5. Are you ready to live an abundant, joyful life?

Feel (in your body) the sensation of a perfect union, or perfect blending with another person and with the All-That-Is.

This section will blend the student's integration of grace into the capacity for faith.

#1. Try a blending experience. In meditation, a quiet state of mind, imagine yourself being lifted, your vibration picking up speed. Imagine your energies blending with very, very fine fifth dimensional frequencies. What does this experience do for you?

#2. What have been the reactions of other people in your life lately when they are around you? When you resonate a frequency of grace, is the environment and/or relationship different than it was before you began working consciously with the energy of grace?

#3. Do you have compassion? Do you feel compassion? What stirs your compassion?

#4. Do you understand time lapses in faith? (Meaning that there is often time between wishing something into manifestation and the actual manifestation itself.) How do you work with these time lapses?

#5. Do you have faith? How does faith work for you?

GRACE
Section 9: Believing

The primary purpose of this section is to assist light workers in integrating faith so completely that it becomes an integral part of the personal belief system, no longer external but a part of experience.

#1. Explain what it is like for you (what it feels like or what the experience is like) to be in third dimensional reality and then again in multi-dimensional consciousness regarding levels of faith and belief.

In other words, how is your faith or belief in the All-That-Is changed by where your personal perception is at any given time? (3-D or M-D)

#2. Focus on personal situations in your present experience that are not as satisfying as you would like them to be. Are your thoughts primarily focused on lack of something in this situation? Do you often think about "not having" regarding these situations? What sensations would you experience if you were to have that which you desire?

When you have answered these questions thoroughly, take a moment and meditate upon fulfillment. Actually feel within your body what it would be like to have all needs fulfilled. Be with that sensation for a time. This will allow your bodies (physical, emotional, and mental bodies) to Know what fulfillment is in order that they may eventually manifest such.

#3. Think about a desire in your past that has been granted. Did you receive the gift with grace? Did the desire come to you with ease or with struggle? Did you have appreciation for the gift granted? How open are you to receiving?

#4. Do you find it easy to surrender?

#5. Do you believe that everything you desire, you can create?

Prioritize a list of desires at this time and review it periodically.

Section 10: Higher Guidance and Intention

The power of intention will clench the Segment on Grace for the student.

Compose a personal statement that clarifies your intention to live and love in grace. Use this intention when waking each morning and when transmitting to other persons and the planet.

Take time to meditate daily, recording any guidance received —insights, thoughts, dreams, etc. You may use these pages as your Daily Meditation Log.

DAILY MEDITATION LOG

MULTI-DIMENSIONAL LIVING
Section 1a: Understanding Multi-Dimensional Living

Section 1a and 1b assist the student with tapping into the multi-dimensional perception and experience. Section 1a discusses understanding. Section 1b relates to perception.

#1. In the next nine to twelve months, what do you expect to happen in your life?

This manuscript was transcribed (channeled) with the intention to reach the individual student. As you are reading this material, the information will be pertinent to you in the moment. If you review it in one year it will most likely still be relevant to your process but the words may be interpreted differently and have a more expansive meaning to you.

#2. Where does your imagination take you? Do you have doubt regarding these imaginings?

#3. Do you understand how to manifest from the heart center, instead of from desirous thought or ego? Explain how you feel about manifesting this way (from the heart).

#4. What are you depriving yourself of? Would you be able to accept this (these things; relationships, situations, experiences) into your world if you were thus given them?

#5. What does it mean to you to participate, yet to remain in observer mode?

#1. "Follow flow without resistance." What may be your resistance, if any?

#2. List the three most important things you wish to manifest at this time? Will these desires (once manifested) distract you from your connection to the Highest Self?

#3. Focus through soul (a multi-dimensional perception) looking at your present experience. First look at it rationally, then through your emotion. How does the situation honestly make you feel? Then look through the eyes of your soul. What "soul" purpose does your present experience hold for you?

The intention of these questions is to repeatedly prompt you to always look at the multi-dimensional purpose of all experience.

#4. Are there various levels of this particular (or one) experience that can give you insight to the whole of your present life?

Go into deep levels of understanding to ascertain why particular events/experiences happen when they do.

#5. Does this way of perceiving feel more pleasant (or perhaps even ecstatic) than your previous way of perceiving?

This section brings the student to an understanding of how important it is to clear physical energies and to heal the physical body (ridding it) of fear and the causes of illness.

#1. Begin by quietly looking at any fear you might have in your body. Examine what fear does to the body. Does it make your body tense or anxious? Now, if you can begin to sense ecstasy in your own way. What does ecstasy feel like to you? Stay with this feeling as long as you can. If you are unable to sense ecstasy, just imagine what it might be like. Explain your understanding.

#2. Raising your physical vibration. Can you feel a shift when you consciously imagine your vibration rising? What changes does this make in your experience?

#3. What types of shifts have you been through in the last two years?

#4. How do you tend to your physical body's needs? Is there more that you can do to"take care?"

#5. What is your reaction to "the physical is Divine?"

Loving Self is key to ascension. To get back into God's favor. Students of the ascension will get in touch with Self and eliminate that which hinders Self development.

#1. When you focus your attention on the psychic stratum (the layer between the fifth and sixth dimension) what do you see, sense or feel? Are other people using this stratum to manipulate you?

Use the meditation strategy in **"RELEASING AND UTILIZING PSYCHIC INFLUENCES"**

#2. What do you experience after a "cleansing of the psyche" meditation?

#3. Do you love yourself?

#4. Are you ready to renounce all that which controls your life without your permission?

#5. When answering question #4, is there any doubt or fear that comes up for you?

This section prepares students for the world experience ahead. The ascension process is underway and with the questions that follow the path is solidified and made clearer.

#1. Take a look at the people you associate with. Do you enjoy their company? Do you feel good and light-filled when you are with them? Are there some that you need to associate with less or transmit more light to?

#2. How easy is it for you to "go with the flow"? To go with what FEELS right?

#3. Do you ask for proof? Has proof been presented to you? Can you let go of needing proof?

#4. Do you trust your intuition?

#5. When in prayer, can you get to a place of true reverence for the power of Creation? Also, what does this reverence do for your mood?

Section 5: Linearity and Layers in Consciousness

This section will open the student to the awareness of more beyond the third dimension. It juts into the consciousness of other dimensions.

#1. An experiment with light can produce interesting results. What happens when you work with light in meditation? Do you see or sense the mental gridwork around and through you and the planet?

#2. When you KNOW in your heart (your feeling center, your intuition) that something is right or wrong for you, do you often back it up with linear analysis? Explain a situation where you have done this. This will help in the building process of your manifestation.

#3. Do you understand the imagery of the outer shell ? What assists you in penetrating this shell and removing the illusionary concept that the third dimensional perception is the one and only reality?

#4. What is your understanding of each of the layers of consciousness ?

This section will assist the student in using imagination and work on the mental gridwork to purify Creation and manifest in the physical.

#1. "The imagination is the gel that connects all matter with non-matter." Do you have resistance to this statement? Do you have ultimate trust in your fantasy?...in your intuition? Do you believe that these imaginings can become real?

#2. What in your life, in your experience, would you like to change? Can you imagine how the new experience will look?

#3. Do you have desires based on emotional longing? Contemplate your desires, delve into them to find out the deepest, most subconscious connection to this desire and from where it might stem.

#4. Imagine the gridwork. What do you see? After working in meditation to clear and beautify the gridwork, what happens (if anything) to your energy?

#5. How do you feel about adjusting or working on the gridwork to serve others?

#5. As you find love expanding within your realm of awareness (as you progress with this material and work with the layers in consciousness), what type of reactions are your bodies (physical, emotional, mental) displaying?

This section is the student's first intense experience thus far in utilizing Light Work technique directly.

#1. Begin the meditation on **Blasting**. Do you notice open spaces within your being? Fill them with a sense of love energy. Do you notice any changes?

#2. Second meditation (**cylinder** visualization). How do you experience the cylinder? And the pinpoint of light?

#3. How do you experience your light body? (the body of energy/light extending beyond your auric body)

#4. When you BLAST what happens?

#5. Having done some light work, now do you see any significant changes in your experience? How so?

The student will thoroughly begin to become familiar with experiencing energy in this section and will know how it works in Creation.

#1. Explain in your own words that place of KNOWING. How is that for you?

#2. Think of one thing, i.e. experience, situation, material object that you KNOW you desire. Let go of the longing and just concentrate mentally on this thing. Analyze how it is that you KNOW you want this particular thing in your life. Break the essence of this apart bit by bit to understand and thoroughly KNOW and trust this KNOWING.

#3. What is your experience with <u>liquid</u> <u>love</u> or any other frequencies or energy patterns?

#4. How easy is it for you to let go of the past and surrender to the flow?

#5. When you bring the essence energy of your future into the now, what happens? Describe the energy sensation or whatever you get.

MULTI-DIMENSIONAL LIVING
Section 9: Societal Changes/Time and Space

This section brings students to the awareness of earth changes and how they effect society and the concept of time sequencing, the flow.

#1. Are you experiencing the shifts in vibration of the earth? How so? Do you see evidence of earth changes in your experience? Do you recognize changes within yourself, in your relationships, in your experience?

#2. What types of changes (go into very subtle detail with this question) do you see in your work? Would you say that you are a pillar (a Light Worker working within an established institution) or do you do your light work mostly from the outside? Do you need to make any changes accordingly?

#3. Try an experiment: Go without a watch for one day. What is this like for you?

#4. Do you ever experience "no time", a segment of time which seems to have disappeared? Explain what you experience. How does it get there? How abruptly does it end and what is going on in between?

#5. Practice with time, slowing it down or speeding it up. Most generally to shorten lag time in creation, one must slow time down into long, tedious moments. This will help you to understand time. Once understood, it begins to move in an even fashion.

MULTI-DIMENSIONAL LIVING
Section 10: The Twelve Manifestation Principles

This section takes the student into the Twelve Mysteries as instructed by the Naguda Force. Familiarity with these lessons will allow for integration of all of the *Dimensional Ascension* material.

#1. ALWAYS FOLLOW UNIVERSAL LAW (SPIRIT LAW) BEFORE HUMAN MADE LAW.
Do you recognize the difference? Can you make this a permanent fixture in your reality?

#2. LAW OF DETACHMENT
Can you detach from everything, even your personality? What is this like for you?

#3. YOU ARE MANIFESTING ILLUSION NOT REALITY
Reaction?

#4. LAW OF FOCUS
Practice regular meditation.

#5. UNLEASHING THE THIRD DIMENSIONAL LAW OF VICTIMIZATION
How are you [allowing yourself to be] victimized?

#6. LAW OF DESERVEDNESS
Do you feel deserving of great abundance? Do you see the aura of the material world changing?

#7. LAW OF CONFIDENTIALITY ATTRACTION
Do you have enough confidence to attract all of what you want?

#8. BECOMING THE SOUL SELF EMBODIED
As you spiral your personality self into light, record your experiences.

#9. SEEING EVERYTHING AS ENERGY
Open your eyes (perception) to a wider consciousness seeing everything, absolutely everything as energy.

#10. ENERGY IN MOTION (E-MOTION)
Try moving the energy when you are stuck in an emotion you do not like.

#11. UNIVERSAL SELF SUFFICIENCY
Do you now remember who you are and what power you have?

#12. THE EXQUISITE LAW OF MASCULINE & FEMININE BALANCE
How have each of these energies worked for you in your life and are you experiencing more blending in recent days?

LOVE AND RELATIONSHIP
Section 1: Relationship

In this section, students are encouraged to make a thorough inventory of personal and professional relationships, including relationship with self.

#1. How satisfied are you to be alone? If you have rarely been alone for an extended period of time, how do you think you would handle it? Be very clear, very specific as to your personal needs and to what you would want out of a relationship.

#2. List ten ideals you would like to have (or do have) in relationship?

#3. Bring the love frequency into your body. Feel love within and share it with others throughout your day. How does this turn out for you?

#4. How easily do you receive (accept) love coming from others? Recognize your reactions when you send out love and receive it in return.

#5. Do you recognize any hierarchical relations in your experience? How has this affected the way you give and receive love?

LOVE AND RELATIONSHIP
Section 2: Love

Students get in touch with love and all it has to offer in this section.

#1. Think about situations or people that you "hate" or strongly dislike. Do you experience the love in this once you remove the anger? What is it about this object, situation, or person that makes you angry? Do you want to detach from it/them so as to be dispassionate toward it/them?

#2. Strength plus freedom and unity as one. You can not have complete union with another until you are free within. Comment on this.

#3. Do you trust yourself? Does trust come up as an issue in any of your relationships? How so? Is this a reflection, past or present, or an out-picturing of something within you?

#4. Meditate on what love feels like within. Can you create healing by focusing on love? Can you erase guilt by experiencing more love?

#5. When you are at peace what happens? Do you then trust the higher flow?

It is very important to experience and KNOW compassion before moving on to Soul Mated Relationship.

#1. Can you feel compassion (that deep, very intense love)? How do you experience compassion?

#2. Make a list of everything for which you feel compassion.

#3. Think of someone close to you. In your mind's eye, picture his or her soul body in front of you. Now experience compassion within and transmit it to that other person. Describe this experience. Make note of how your relationship with that person changes after you do this exercise.

#4. Ask questions of another in meditation. Ask your own soul questions. What answers do you get?

#5. Meditate on what love feels like within. Can you create healing by focusing on love? Can you erase guilt by experiencing more love?

LOVE AND RELATIONSHIPS
Section 4: Soul Mated Relationship

Learning to sense the energy of the soul mate takes time in this third dimensional perception. In this section students learn to recognize and accept the soul mate experience.

#1. Do you know (one or more of) your soul mate/s? If so, do you see how your soul energy resonates compatibly with your soul mate? If you do not know your soul mate, imagine in your mind's eye the experience of this person's energy.

#2. What do you expect or want to experience through a soul mated relationship?

#3. Describe any power struggles that you may now be experiencing in any relationship. Do you find that the conflict is a necessary one still for learning, or can you release it?

#4. After you cleanse your emotional body (via meditation, a good cry, journaling, etc.), what do you experience?

#5. Do you sense your personal frequencies? Can you sense the passion that awaits?

Section 5: TRANSCENDENCE JOURNEY

Do the Transcendence Journey and record notes.

<u>**Transcendence Journey Notes**</u>

Do the journey (meditation) several times and record responses.

SPIRAL JOURNEY NOTES

<u>Dimensional Ascension: Multi-Dimensional Living for Light Workers</u> is book number one in the Utopian Vision Ascension Series, followed by <u>Sexual Ascension: Love and Intimacy for Spiritual Beings</u>.

If you would like to host an Intensive Focus Group (extended weekend retreat or online discussion) based on the *Dimensional Ascension* material and facilitated by Jules Kennedy, please contact us through our website: <u>www.utopianvision.com</u>

The Utopian Vision came into being as a third dimensional construct to bring forward universal TRUTH from various realms, dimensions, experiences and beings. Through the mediums of the written word, lectures, seminars and individual counseling, The Utopian Vision facilitates and assists individuals in grounding this truth in their hearts. The Utopian Vision is expanding its vision to meet the upcoming needs of this changing world consciousness.

Jules Kennedy has been teaching, counseling, and writing in the areas of metaphysics, spirituality, the occult and Ascension since 1984. She holds degrees in Human Development, Counseling, and Psychic Studies. She has pursued a diverse career path in social work, volunteer administration, counseling, and psychic advising and teaching. She has been channeling information from many sources since childhood but officially since 1987. She has clientele and students worldwide. She currently does psychic advising and business consulting by phone and email, and teaches at various metaphysical events. She also puts out a quarterly newsletter of channeled material and has implemented *The Utopian Vision*, the business foundation that holds a concrete space for this Ascension Work to take form in this world.

Private readings and/or consulting sessions with Jules Kennedy are available through her website: <u>www.juleskennedy.com</u>.

Made in the USA
Columbia, SC
17 November 2018